CONVERSATIONS WITH TOSCANINI

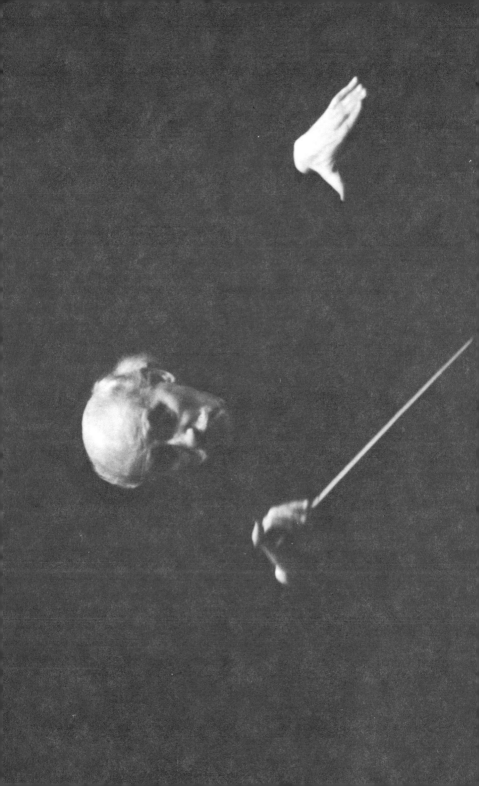

B.H. HAGGIN

Conversations with Toscanini

SECOND EDITION

Enlarged

HORIZON PRESS • New York • 1979

The photograph facing the title-page and the photographs on pages 108 and 109 are from This Was Toscanini by Samuel Antek published by The Vanguard Press. Photographs copyright © 1963 by Robert Hupka.

CONTENTS

Foreword   8

  1.Conversations with Toscanini   9

ADDENDA

  2.Rehearsals and Performances of the Last Years   95

  3.Photographs and Letters   108

  4.Postscript—1979   119

  5.The Toscanini Recordings—1979   144

  6.The Writing About Toscanini   162

APPENDIX: Article—"Genius Betrayed"   169

Acknowledgements   178

CONVERSATIONS WITH TOSCANINI

FOREWORD

This new edition, until the top of page 107, duplicates exactly the text published in 1959, retaining the "A——" on pages 60, 66 and 80 that in 1959 referred to Munch, the "X——" on page 28 that referred to Beecham, the "Y——" on page 57 that referred to Rodzinski, and the "Z——" on page 60 that referred to Reiner—all of whom were then still alive. The rest is new writing concerned with what I learned in the years since 1959 about Toscanini's "resignation" from the NBC Symphony and his broadcasts and recordings; with the recordings available today; and with the writing about him.

1

CONVERSATIONS WITH TOSCANINI

Once, after a rehearsal at which Toscanini had erupted into one of his rages, I heard an NBC Symphony player ask Harry Glantz, the orchestra's first trumpet who had played under Toscanini in the New York Philharmonic: "Was he any worse in his Philharmonic days?"

"Well," said Glantz with a meaningful look, "he was fifteen years younger."

The fact is that Toscanini did mellow in his later years; and it is to this fact, I am sure, that I owe the personal experiences with him that I am about to describe. For from the very beginning of my awareness of his existence—which is to say from January 1914, when I heard my first performance at the Metropolitan, one of *Madama Butterfly* which he conducted—he was for me an awesome figure, known to be formidable to the musicians whom he worked with in the opera house, and remote, forbidding, unapproachable outside of the opera house—unapproachable above all to the press (though one of the newspaper reviewers, Max Smith, was a personal friend). And this impression of him was strengthened in the course of time by the excitement over his sudden, silent, unexplained, and therefore mysterious departure from the Metropolitan in April 1915; the excitement over his return in the season of 1920–21 for a tour with the orchestra of La Scala; the excitement over his coming as guest conductor to the New York Philharmonic in January 1926; the excitement over his departure—again silent and mysterious—from the New York Philharmonic-Symphony in 1936; the excitement over his performances in Salzburg in 1937.

Toscanini's awesomeness was brought home to me personally in one particular way. My piano teacher at the Institute of Musical Art had known some of the wealthy women who were influential in the affairs of New York orchestras; and I had been given permission to attend Mengelberg's rehearsals first with the National Symphony and then with the New York Philharmonic. Some of these women also came to the rehearsals; and Mengelberg seemed to enjoy having a little audience for his lectures to the orchestra on what he called the "princips" of orchestral performance. But with Toscanini nobody was allowed at rehearsals; and one read about the lights being turned on periodically in Carnegie Hall while the staff went through the balconies to make sure nobody was hiding up there. Under these circumstances I didn't even try to get in; but I must have learned things were different in Salzburg, for in 1937, when I was about to go there, I secured, through the kindness of Mr. B. W. Huebsch, a letter from Stefan Zweig to Mme. Toscanini asking permission for me to attend one rehearsal. In Salzburg, in obedience to Zweig's instructions, I presented myself to a specified intermediary who took me to the *Festspielhaus* where we waited for Mme. Toscanini to come out; and I was then presented to her and gave her the letter. She asked which rehearsal I would like to attend, and I said one of Verdi's *Requiem*; and she said I would hear from her at the proper time, a few weeks later; but I never did. By this time I had—as someone who was keeping the AP correspondent in Vienna informed of what was happening in Salzburg—become *persona grata* to the director of the festival; and from him I obtained a pass to the last rehearsal for Toscanini's last orchestral concert. But when I got to the *Festspielhaus* I found a little group of Toscanini relatives and friends standing outside disconsolately: enraged by something that had gone wrong in the rehearsal the day before, he had decreed that nobody was to be allowed in today.

The excitement over Toscanini's return to New York in December 1937 to conduct the NBC Symphony did not make him a less awesome and remote figure for me. And I was therefore wholly unprepared for what happened in Carnegie Hall one Sunday afternoon in March 1940. Sauntering down the aisle, Robert A. Simon of *The New Yorker* stopped to ask: "Do you know Toscanini reads you in *The Nation?*" Amazed, I answered: "No. How do *you* know?" "People who see him have told me," said Simon. "He showed them your article on the Philharmonic and Barbirolli and said: 'See?'"

Actually the article Simon referred to had been not about the Philharmonic and Barbirolli but about how certain critics had dealt with the subject. I had pointed out how W. J. Henderson's crotchety irritation with the fuss about virtuoso conductors had caused him to insist in the *Sun* that the Philharmonic and the music of Beethoven and Brahms would remain even without Toscanini and even with a conductor of less than stellar magnitude, though he must have known that the orchestra and the music would sound different under such a conductor; and how this had placed a powerful argument in the hands of those who had brought about the engagement of Barbirolli, which had considerably reduced the orchestra's usefulness to the community. I had pointed out further that Henderson had at least—when he had heard subsequently what the Philharmonic and the music actually sounded like under Barbirolli's direction—expressed his disapproval; whereas Lawrence Gilman had written in the *Herald Tribune* concerning Barbirolli's achievements—including a performance of Brahms's Fourth which had torn passion to tatters—that they showed him to be "something better and rarer and finer than a conductor of power and sensibility. He permits us to think that he is akin to those uncommon interpreters who give us a measure of 'that inner standard of distinction, selection, refusal' which an incorruptible artist once defined: who have sifted from experience 'all that seemed beautiful and significant, and have treasured above all things those savings of fine gold.'" And I had said that in this way Gilman had been of great help to the Philharmonic directors—"the help, perhaps, that an orchestra's program annotator should be; but he failed in his obligations to his position as critic, to his readers, to the community whose orchestra the Philharmonic was." All this apparently had been of interest to Toscanini; and his "See?" carried implications of how he had felt about it.

I was pleased of course by what Simon told me; but it

wasn't until a year later that it gave me the courage to write Toscanini for what I considered a legitimate purpose: to suggest that he perform Berlioz's *L'Enfance du Christ*, which W. J. Turner had declared to be Berlioz's most beautiful score, but which at that time was never performed. I wrote Toscanini that I addressed my request to him because of the interest in Berlioz he had shown by playing *Harold in Italy* and the *Queen Mab* Scherzo and other excerpts from *Romeo and Juliet*; because it had been in *Harold* as he had performed it around 1930 that I had first understood the special quality of Berlioz's mind, imagination and style; and because what I was asking was something for the entire musical public: it was like asking someone to let the public see a great painting that had been hidden for many years. And I added a request that he conduct and record *Queen Mab*.

Some days later, opening an envelope addressed in an unfamiliar and striking handwriting, and unfolding the letter inside it, I was amazed again to see at the bottom of the sheet, signed very cordially, the name Arturo Toscanini. Evidently under the impression that I had suggested *L'Enfance du Christ* for the broadcast of April 5, he wrote that he was sorry but the program for that date had already been planned as follows: Rossini's Overture to *Il Signor Bruschino*, Mendelssohn's *Scotch* Symphony, and Berlioz's Overture *Les Francs-Juges*, his *Love Scene* and *Queen Mab* from *Romeo and Juliet*, and his Hungarian March from *The Damnation of Faust*. And he assured me *Queen Mab* would be recorded.

I wrote to thank him for his kindness in answering me, and to express my hope that he would perform *L'Enfance* at a later time—which he never did.

In November 1941 I wrote to him again. He was to conduct the Philadelphia Orchestra in three programs that season, and Victor had announced some of the performances would be recorded. I told him that I had had his 1936 performance of Schubert's C-major Symphony with the New York Philharmonic recorded off the air, but that the recording had turned out to be imperfect, and that I therefore hoped this symphony would be one of the works he would record for Victor. I hoped also for recordings of Tchaikovsky's *Pathétique* and *Romeo and Juliet,* of Mozart and Haydn, and of course Berlioz's *Queen Mab.* And I wrote that I had learned from his son that he had disliked what I had written about Brahms in my *Book of the Symphony,* but that possibly he would like what I had written about Mozart, Haydn, Schubert, Tchaikovsky in my new book *Music on Records.*

This brought a reply in which Toscanini informed me that one of his first recordings would be the Schubert C-major Symphony which he was going to conduct the following week with the Philadelphia Orchestra, and that he would record also the *Pathétique, Ibéria* and *Queen Mab.* Then, for no reason, apparently, other than the fact that it was in his mind at the moment, he went on to say he had a weakness for Beethoven's Septet, which he had played the preceding season with ten violins, ten violas, eight cellos and four basses, because he had never enjoyed this wonderful music when it was played by seven instruments as Beethoven wrote it. He had, he said, heard many performances of the piece in its original form by distinguished musicians; but the right balance [of strings and three winds] had never been attained. He would, he went on, read what I said about Schubert, Haydn and Mozart with the utmost interest; concerning Brahms his comment was, for the moment, the Italian proverb *acqua in bocca.* And he ended with cordial greetings.

The Schubert C-major opened the first program, which I heard at the Saturday-night concert of the pair on November 15. The performance of the symphony was of course the matter of major interest; but interesting too was the way the orchestra played and sounded under Toscanini's direction. Since 1937 he had been working with the NBC Symphony, and producing with it excitingly beautiful and effective performances but not the sheer incandescence of execution and sonority that he had achieved with the New York Philharmonic; and the reason for this was not, as some have contended recently, that he could conduct orchestras but not build and train them. "You can quote me on this," said an NBC Symphony violinist in happy excitement once after a rehearsal of Debussy's *La Mer,* at the end of which the orchestra had applauded Toscanini: "We come here to go to school!" And the contention—by some who never even heard the Philharmonic under either Mengelberg or Toscanini—that it was not Toscanini but Mengelberg who made of this orchestra an ensemble in the class of Stokowski's Philadelphia and Koussevitzky's Boston Symphony, is contrary to the facts that I observed. I was a witness, at the daily rehearsals, of the training Mengelberg gave the Philharmonic from 1921 to 1926, and can testify to the discipline and finish of its playing under his direction; but although I did not witness Toscanini's work at rehearsals I did hear that it was only when the orchestra began to play under him in 1926 that it began to exhibit the dazzling virtuosity and tonal beauty comparable with those of the Philadelphia and Boston Symphony—to produce, that is, the razor-sharp attacks, the sharp-contoured phrases, the radiant sonorities and transparent textures comparable with the Philadelphia's lush sumptuousness, the Boston Symphony's refinement of execution and tone. Moreover it was Toscanini who in 1928 chose the players from the Philharmonic and the New York Symphony for the combined Philharmonic-Symphony, and who trained this orchestra to the point where its playing exhibited the incandescence I have mentioned, which can be heard in the 1936 recordings of the Rossini Overtures to *Semiramide* and *L'Italiana in Algeri* and the Brahms-Haydn Variations.

If now it is asked what *was* the reason why the Philharmonic could play in this way and the NBC Symphony could not, the answer is that the Philharmonic was a group of players who had worked together for a number of years, whose only professional activity was playing together as a symphony orchestra, and who—whatever the laxity they permitted themselves with other conductors—maintained in their four or five rehearsals and three or four concerts each week with Toscanini the discipline, cohesiveness, and sensitiveness to his direction that they had acquired in their years of work with him; whereas the NBC Symphony had been assembled only a couple of months before Toscanini began to conduct it, and the nature and conditions of its members' other work largely nullified the training he gave it. NBC did not in 1937 create an additional new orchestra for Toscanini's exclusive use: it had a staff orchestra for its Red and Blue Networks, and the NBC Symphony was set up as a group within that staff orchestra—a group which included a number of players engaged for Toscanini as higher-caliber replacements of previous members of the staff orchestra. The weekly "services" of the NBC Symphony players were therefore not merely the up to ten hours of rehearsal and the hour-and-a-half broadcast with Toscanini: they included also more than that number of hours of rehearsal and performance for the networks' other programs, sustaining and commercial, with conductors unable to hold the players to Toscanini's high technical and musical standards; and he had to work with men who sometimes came to his rehearsal straight from a two-hour rehearsal of dance music, or rushed from his rehearsal to a commercial program under a staff conductor. And later, after NBC had had to sell the Blue Network, the NBC Symphony was made up of (1) a permanent group of about forty-five who were part of the NBC staff orchestra of sixty-five that included about twenty men used in jazz programs, and (2) about forty-five extra men engaged only for the NBC Symphony series, who were not always the same; and members of the jazz contingent also were used on occasion. Hence it was not until 1950, and the transcontinental tour that gave the orchestra six weeks of rehearsing and playing under Toscanini, that it began to exhibit the precise, finished and sensitive execution, the blending, refinement and beauty of tone, of a first-rate symphony orchestra.

In Philadelphia in November 1941, therefore, after Toscanini's four years with the NBC house orchestra, it was interesting to hear what he achieved with one of the world's great symphony orchestras again—this time with the marvelous instrument Stokowski had created in the Philadelphia Orchestra. One thing that was interesting was the change in the orchestra's playing: instead of the Stokowski flood of tonal sumptuousness and splendor it produced the Toscanini radiance, transparency, sharpness of attack and contour. But it was interesting also that playing under Toscanini only a few days the orchestra was not sensitized to his direction as the Philharmonic had been after ten years, so that he didn't get from it the miraculous subtleties of inflection and coloring of the

Philharmonic's 1936 *Semiramide* performance. And there was in addition a human aspect of the occasion that was touching: Stokowski had left the orchestra a few years earlier; and the awe on the face of the very young first cellist, Samuel Mayes, as he looked up from his music to Toscanini during the Schubert symphony, the smiles of all the men at the end of the performance, were evidence of what it meant to them to be playing again under a great conductor, and one who was in addition a great musician.

But what was most important was the performance of the symphony. The work was very dear to Toscanini (he played it at his very first orchestral concert, on March 20, 1896, in Turin); and his treatment of it had always been criticized— one of the things objected to being his faster-than-usual tempo for the second movement. I had always been startled by the first measures and had then gone along easily with the rest of the movement; but at this Philadelphia performance I thought I understood for the first time what was behind that fast tempo: a feeling for plastic simplicity, economy, subtlety, that caused Toscanini often to set a single subtly modified tempo for all the sections of a movement. In the second movement of the Schubert C-major, then, he set a tempo for the opening section that he could maintain unchanged not only for the alternating section but for the catastrophe in the middle of the movement, so that the increasing urgency and tension of this passage was achieved without any acceleration, and in fact a slight broadening at the end gave shattering power to the chords with which the passage breaks off into momentary silence.

It was also objected that Toscanini's performance was not in the Viennese tradition—which led me to question such tradition and its authority. Even if Schubert had himself conducted a performance of his C-major Symphony which conductors of his time had heard and followed as a model for their own performances, which in turn had been followed as models by their successors, and so on down to the present— even if all this had happened I did not believe that what Schubert had done with the symphony would be still discernible in the performances today. But actually the symphony

was rehearsed but not performed shortly after his death; then
it was forgotten until Schumann discovered it in 1838 and
Mendelssohn played it in 1839; and these performances represented only the understanding of the work that each conductor had achieved by his own study of the score. Did this
establish a tradition which could forbid other musicians—and
one of the greatest musicians of all time—to do the same thing?
(I asked this unaware that Richard Strauss, asking who could
maintain today that Beethoven did or did not want a particular tempo, had contended there was no tradition determining
such matters and the personal artistic conviction of the conductor had to decide what was right or wrong.)

Another objection was that this symphony was a Viennese
work which should be played with a Viennese relaxation that
Toscanini's performance did not have. But not all the music
written in Vienna is alike, and not all of it is relaxed: the
particular relaxed quality of some of Schubert's music is not
in Mozart's or Beethoven's or even all of Schubert's. A correct
understanding of his music includes perception of the power
and tension in some of it; and a correct understanding of the
C-major Symphony includes perception of its sustained tension and momentum and grandeur, which Toscanini's performance achieved as no other did.

In addition to the Schubert, Toscanini conducted Debussy's
Ibéria and Respighi's *Roman Festivals*; and at the end I went
backstage and talked with a member of the orchestra whom
I knew. After a while I caught sight of Walter Toscanini; and
I asked him if I might thank his father. "Certainly," he replied. "He reads you; he answers your letters; he doesn't answer *my* letters but he answers *yours*"; and smiling he led me
to his father's dressing room. When we got there Toscanini
and Mme. Toscanini were standing in the doorway saying
good-by to the last visitor, and Mme. Toscanini was about
to close the door. "This is Mr. Haggin of *The Nation*," said
Walter to his father, who smiled and extended his hand but
said nothing; and I thanked him and left.

I went to Philadelphia again for the concert of January 10,
1942, at which Toscanini conducted Haydn's Symphony No.
99, Respighi's orchestration of Bach's *Passacaglia* for organ,

excerpts from Mendelssohn's music for A *Midsummer Night's Dream*, and Strauss's *Death and Transfiguration*. When I saw Walter Toscanini at the end of the concert he said: "Father did not know who you were last time. He said: 'Why you did not tell me it was Mr. Haggin of *The Nation?*'" And he led me again to his father's dressing room, which this time was filled with visitors. But when Walter introduced me to him Toscanini again smiled and extended his hand and said nothing. There was an exchange in Italian between Walter and his father; then, as Toscanini was drawn away by someone else, Walter said to me: "Father said about your new book: 'He writes like God: he knows what is good music and what is bad music. I do not know what is good music and what is bad music; but *he* knows.'" °

Before I went to Philadelphia for the concert of February 7 I was told I could be present at the recording session the following day. At the concert Toscanini conducted Tchaikovsky's *Pathétique*, a Vieuxtemps Ballade and Polonaise, Berlioz's *Queen Mab*, and Debussy's *La Mer*; and the next day I was present during the recording of the *Pathétique* and part of *La Mer*. The occasion provided my first experience of Toscanini rehearsing—of which I remember now only his working out dynamic values and balances in the introduction of the *Pathétique*.

During a break in the recording session, Walter invited me to visit his father in his dressing room, where we found him fanning himself and worrying about the difficulties of recording. "I make *pianissimo* in *La Mer*: in hall is correct; on record is *not* correct! In 1936 I make *Rhine Journey* with Philharmonic. I go to Paris; a commission—Gilman, Betti, Chotzinoff[1]—listen to record and say is good. In Carnegie Hall is right tempo; when I hear record, is wrong tempo. Last year I am in bed, and a friend telephone to me: 'Maestro, listen to

° (1979) Some readers didn't understand that Toscanini was speaking facetiously.

[1] (1979) In 1936 Lawrence Gilman had been the music critic of the New York *Herald Tribune*; Adolfo Betti the first violin of the Flonzaley Quartet; Samuel Chotzinoff the music critic of the New York *Post*. In 1959 Bruno Zirato of the New York Philharmonic informed me that Chotzinoff had not been a member of the committee that listened to the recordings.

radio.' I listen: is *Rhine Journey*; is good—is right tempo—IS MY *RHINE JOURNEY!* in 1936 is wrong tempo; now is right tempo! Ah, *Dio santo!*" and he hurled the fan at the wall in despair.

The program was repeated in New York two days later—which is to say after the additional rehearsal and playing at the recording sessions—and in Carnegie Hall, which was acoustically even finer than the Academy of Music; with the result that the sounds produced by the orchestra on this occasion ranged themselves with the other wonders I had heard achieved by human powers in Carnegie Hall—the sounds produced by the Philadelphia Orchestra under Stokowski, the Boston Symphony under Koussevitzky, the New York Philharmonic under Toscanini. But the sounds were not just sounds: they added up to wonderfully right and effective realizations of the pieces of music; and it seemed to me that one reason for the impression of rightness conveyed at every point in the progression of the first movement of Tchaikovsky's *Pathétique* was the plastic coherence imparted to the form in sound by Toscanini's sense for continuity and proportion in the continuum of sound moving in time; and that another reason was the fact that the nuances of sonority and tempo with which he molded this continuum were the ones Tchaikovsky specified in his score to produce the form he had imagined. Or rather, they were the close approximations to these that a performer could achieve: the composer's notations could not convey the imagined form completely; the performer therefore could not produce it in living sound exactly as the composer had imagined it; and his obligation was to produce it to the extent to which the notation did convey it. About halfway through the first movement of Debussy's *La Mer*, after the music has died down into mutterings of basses and kettledrums, an upward leap of the cellos is followed by a slight swell of the kettledrum from *pp* to *p* and back, and this by an echoing swell of the horns. There was no notation that could convey exactly what Debussy imagined as *pp* and *p* and as the timbres of the horns; and his notation therefore left room for the differences between Toscanini's values for *pp* and *p* and Koussevitzky's, the sound of Toscanini's horns and that of Koussevitzky's; but it left no room for Koussevitzky's change of the swell of kettledrum followed by echoing swell of horns to the simultaneous thunderous swell of kettledrum *and* horns. For Koussevitzky a person who wanted the composer's score adhered to was someone who didn't want the music to be alive (the words are his); but it was Toscanini who, by obeying Debussy's directions, gave life to the magical effect of horns echoing over the water, and it was Koussevitzky who, by his change, killed that effect.

In April 1942 the New York Philharmonic ended its centennial season with a Beethoven festival conducted by Toscanini; and I wrote to ask him for permission to attend the rehearsals. He granted it; and so I witnessed the extraordinary thing that happened at the very first rehearsal. It was six years since Toscanini had conducted the orchestra; one expected that it would take inch-by-inch rehearsal to restore the precision and tonal beauty of its playing under him six years earlier; and the members of the orchestra must have expected this too as they sat tuning and practicing passages in the *Missa Solemnis*. Eventually the hubbub died out; there was complete silence as the orchestra waited for Toscanini; and at last he appeared at the side of the stage and, in the tense hush, walked in his absorbed fashion to the podium, stepped onto it, suppressed with a quick gesture the first sounds of a demonstration of welcome, and, with no more than a word of greeting, raised his arm and began to conduct the opening of the *Missa*. And then the extraordinary thing happened: as though the interval had been not six years but one day, the orchestra began at once—in response to the large shaping movements of Toscanini's right arm and the subtly inflecting movements of his left hand—to produce the razor-sharp attacks, the radiant sonorities, the transparent textures, the beautifully contoured phrases which these movements had elicited in April 1936. For minutes at a time he continued to conduct and the orchestra continued to play in this way; only after such long stretches were there halts to go back and correct an imperfect balance at one point or to work out the contour of a phrase at another. And something similar happened at the end of a later rehearsal, when, turning to the finale of the First Symphony, he led the orchestra through it without interruption and produced the performance of six or seven years earlier in all its beautiful detail.

In part, certainly, the explanation of this was Toscanini's powers as a conductor—the movements through which he transmitted his moment-to-moment purpose, the compelling personal force that imposed that purpose through the movements; in part the explanation was the fact that he was conducting an orchestra he had conducted for ten years, and in works they had rehearsed and played together in those years. But I could see that in large part the explanation was the nature of Toscanini's musical conceptions that I mentioned earlier—the plastic continuity and coherence of the shapes he created in the continuum of sound moving in time. That is, in such a progression the timing and force of one sound implied the timing and force of the next irresistibly; and it was the power of these implications, causing the many players in the orchestra to produce the next sound at the same point in time and with the same weight and color, that accounted in large part for the remarkable precision of Toscanini's performances, and for what happened at that first rehearsal of the *Missa*.

Considering these musical conceptions further as musical conceptions, I was struck especially by Toscanini's feeling for the time element in the sound-time continuum; and its manifestations—in his setting of a tempo, his modification of it, his maintenance of proportion between successive tempos —were, it seemed to me, among the most distinctive characteristics of his performances. One heard in the *Missa Solemnis* the rightness of the pace of the *Benedictus* for the blessedness which the music was concerned with, and looking at the score one discovered that this pace was exactly the Andante molto cantabile e non troppo mosso which Beethoven prescribed; but Toscanini didn't get his tempo merely from this direction—he heard it in the music: with the same printed direction, but with not the same musical discernment, Koussevitzky had the *Benedictus* move at an Andante pace so troppo mosso as to be an unsuitable Allegretto. Again, though it was Beethoven who gave only one direction for the entire second movement of the *Eroica* Symphony, it was the necessities of Toscanini's own understanding of the music that caused him alone to establish a single unifying tempo for the various sections. And with no directions at all from Beethoven it was such necessities that produced the subtle modification of this single tempo, the distentions that built up the fugato section of the movement to a climax of shattering power.

A few other incidents of the festival remain in my memory. It was, I believe, after the second rehearsal that Walter Toscanini invited me to visit his father in his dressing room, where we found him radiant. Grasping my coat lapels and giving me a little shake, he said: "My dear Haggin—today I can hope." At a later rehearsal, after devoting considerable time to securing clear articulation of some fast passage-work for strings in the *Leonore* No. 2 Overture, he stopped, undecided, then turned around: "Rachmaninov," he called out, "can you hear?" "I can hear," came the reply from somewhere behind me in the darkened hall; and reassured, Toscanini went on. After the performance of the Ninth Symphony that concluded the festival I went backstage, where I found a huge crowd outside the door of the greenroom. As I stood there Bruno Zirato, at that time assistant manager of the Philharmonic, came out of the room and cast his eye over the crowd; and when he saw me he signaled to me and took me into the room, where Toscanini—wrapped in a blue terry-cloth jacket and fanning himself—stood smiling in the middle of another crowd. When I got near him I thanked him; and he said: "You were not tired to come to all rehearsals?" "If you weren't, why should I be?" I answered. A moment later he asked: "*Qu'est-ce qu'il fait là?*"[2]—motioning toward Walter, who was surrounded by youngsters in uniform. I looked over their shoulders and reported to Toscanini that Walter was taking the names and addresses of the boys who were leaving their programs to be autographed; and he nodded, smiling.

A couple of months later, however, when with other members of the press I attended the final NBC Symphony rehearsal

2 "What is he doing there?"

for the American première of Shostakovitch's Seventh Symphony, I was exhausted after only the first half-hour of the pretentiously inflated banalities. "In this symphony I hear suffering of Russian people," he explained two or three years later, when another symphony of Shostakovitch had appeared in which he said he did not hear anything of interest.

By the autumn of 1942 Toscanini had heard the test pressings of his Philadelphia Orchestra recordings and had been dissatisfied with certain sides, which it was expected he would re-record with the orchestra. (But the long Petrillo ban on recording intervened to prevent the remaking of these sides; in addition the processing of the recordings in incorrectly constituted solutions had resulted in many of the sides being afflicted with noisy ticks; and these were made more disturbing by the excessively low volume-level of the recording. As a result of all these things the recordings—of some of Toscanini's finest performances—were never issued.) I was bringing *Music on Records* up to date for a new edition; and since at this time it was expected that the recordings would eventually be issued (the Berlioz *Queen Mab* was in fact already scheduled for release), I wanted to hear them and list them as being in preparation. I wrote to Walter Toscanini, who was with Victor in Camden, asking if I might hear the test pressings; and he answered that he was going to be in New York the following Monday and would be glad to play for me some that were at his father's home. Would I come to the Villa Pauline between eight-thirty and nine.

The Villa Pauline, in the Riverdale section of New York, was the house Toscanini had lived in since 1937. Shortly after my visit there in September 1942 he moved to the house now occupied by the British delegate to the United Nations; but a few years later he moved back to the Villa Pauline, which remained his American home until his death.

The living room of the Villa Pauline was a large central hall on the ground floor from which a large stairway led to the upper floors. In it, in addition to Walter Toscanini, I found Mme. Toscanini and a young man with whom she was conversing across a small table. She rose to greet me, went to the foot of the stairway, and called softly: "Tosca"; then she returned to the table and her conversation with the young man, which they continued for some time, paying no attention to what else went on in the room. And in a moment Toscanini came down the stairs quickly, a book on world government in one hand, a pince-nez in the other, a smile of greeting on his face.

I had brought with me a recent Victor recording of somebody else's performance of Smetana's *Die Moldau*—excellent-sounding on my phonograph—as a check on the sound of Toscanini's equipment; and I asked Walter to play this first. While I listened to the sound Toscanini stood listening to the performance; and after a few moments he said to Walter: "Get my *Moldau*." Turning to me, he said: "I put trumpet at the end because is not clear only with trombones." When Walter put on the record of a broadcast of *Die Moldau* Toscanini stood not just listening but conducting the performance in every detail; and at the end he directed my attention to the trumpets' strengthening of the melodic line. From this I learned that although Toscanini adhered strictly to the composer's text he didn't hesitate to correct what seemed to him a miscalculation in orchestration that kept something from being heard clearly. (It was surprising to learn, some time later, of the many such changes in *La Mer*. "I tell Debussy are many things not clear; and he say is all right to make changes.")

Toscanini then asked Walter to play the test pressing of an NBC Symphony recording of the Prelude to *Tristan und Isolde* that pleased him with its clarity and sonority; but I found the brilliance of the violins excessive and unpleasant; and when one of the sides of the Philadelphia *Death and Transfiguration* was played I found the violins harsh and the bass too heavy. In reply to my inquiry Walter told me the machine was being played with maximum range of treble and maximum intensity of bass; and I suggested trying the next side of *Death and Transfiguration* with treble range and bass reduced somewhat. This made the violins lustrous and sweet, and changed the bass from a huge confused rumble to sounds that were clearly defined and in correct proportion; and when I said I liked this better Toscanini said he did too. I then

asked to hear the *Tristan* Prelude with my settings of treble
and bass, and found the sound of the violins greatly improved;
but Toscanini this time liked the earlier sound better. However, my settings were retained for the recordings that were
played for me.

One was the Philadelphia *La Mer*, which Toscanini, as before, listened to standing and conducting the performance. At
the end of the first movement, his face registering his delight,
he exclaimed: "Is like reading the score!"—which clearly was
his idea of what a performance should be. Thus he stated
one of his basic principles—that whatever was printed in the
score must be audible in the performance. And a moment
later, listening to the second movement of *La Mer*, he cried
out in anger at not hearing one of the woodwinds, and made
Walter stop the record.

When we came to the Philadephia *Queen Mab* Toscanini's
face clouded, and after asking Walter to bring him the
Wotton book on Berlioz he told me what was troubling him.
He was about to open the New York Philharmonic's season
with a performance of Berlioz's *Romeo and Juliet* in its entirety; and in preparing for it he had again come up against
the problem, for him, of the placing and removal of the
strings' mutes in the *Love Scene*. "A man write to me——" he
said, leaving his statement unfinished as Walter handed him
the Wotton book. "This man," he said, pointing to Wotton's
name, "is musician or is musicologist?" And as I was about to
answer he went on: "I think must be musician"—making clear
in this way his estimate of musicologists. He opened the book
to a passage on page 186, in which he had underlined many
words, and read aloud Wotton's criticism of the reasoning
which had led the editors of the big Breitkopf edition to
change the original direction given on page 151 of the Eulenburg miniature score—the direction to place mutes on the second violins, which the Breitkopf edition extended to violas
and cellos. Then Toscanini showed me in the Eulenburg score
his solution of the problem created, it turned out, not by any
lack of explicitness and clarity in Berlioz's directions but by
Toscanini's inability to believe that they really represented
Berlioz's objectives. On page 147, where Berlioz removed

mutes from the cellos, Toscanini removed them also from the violas; on page 151, where Berlioz added mutes on the second violins to those still on the violas, Toscanini placed them on the second violins, violas and cellos; hence on page 161, where Berlioz removed them from the violas, Toscanini removed them also from the cellos; and instead of removing them from the second violins on page 162 as Berlioz did, Toscanini removed them in the first measure on page 161 because at this point the second violins played the same melody as the unmuted firsts and at the same dynamic level. (The man he said had written to him was Jacques Barzun; but actually it was Toscanini who—encountering Barzun's name in the preface of the Wotton book, and interested in what Barzun might contribute on the subject—had originally written to Barzun. And in his gigantically ostentatious book on Berlioz several years later Barzun wrote that Toscanini had explained his solution of the problem "during a conversation sought"—Barzun informed us —"by him." Toscanini's comment on this was a shake of his head and "Vanity, vanity!")

I remember the playing of only one more recording that night—of the 1941 performance of the finale of *Die Götter-dämmerung* with Helen Traubel. I no longer recall what brought it to Toscanini's mind, and remember only his saying: "You must hear *Immolation Scene* with Traubel. *Ah, che bella voce, che bella voce!*"[3] And he continued to exclaim in pleasure as he listened to what was in fact some of the most beautiful singing of Traubel's career.

A few days later the rehearsals of Berlioz's *Romeo and Juliet* began. Toscanini had played three instrumental sections of the work—the one beginning with *Romeo Alone* and ending with *Great Festivity at the Capulets'*; the *Love Scene*; and the *Queen Mab*—a number of times before; but this performance of the entire work, the first in my lifetime, provided a first hearing of two other extraordinary pieces of music: *Juliet's Funeral Procession* and *Romeo in the Vault of the Capulets*. All this music represented not only Berlioz's re-

---

[3] "Ah, what a beautiful voice, what a beautiful voice!"

markable musical powers but their susceptibility to poetic stimulation; and Toscanini's approach to it was at all times by way of the poetic situation: "Here speaks the prince," he said of the recitative-like passage for the brass in the *Introduction*, which he worked on for the quality and weight of sound, the inflection, the portamento, that made it the pronouncement of an angered ruler. At the point where Romeo's rush—Allegro agitato e disperato—into the Capulet vault broke off, Toscanini's hushing outspread arms and "*Grand silence!*" created the silence of the vault in which were heard the soft, solemn antiphonal chords of brass, woodwinds and strings. And concerning the anguished phrases later in this section he reminded the orchestra: "*DI-SPER-A-TO!* You are all *DI-SPER-A-TI!*"

After the second performance on Friday afternoon I went backstage; but I had stopped to talk to a friend, and when I got to the greenroom I found everyone gone and the door of the dressing room closed. At that moment the door opened and Toscanini came out dressed for the street and followed by Mme. Toscanini. His mind was still on Berlioz's music; and when I spoke of how extraordinary *Romeo in the Vault of the Capulets* was, he answered with an intense "Ye-e-es!" and added: "One finds in Berlioz's scores some things one cannot understand or imagine—until one hears them from the orchestra; then one hears they are right and beautiful."

For his second week's concerts with the Philharmonic Toscanini's program comprised Haydn's Symphony No. 99 and Shostakovitch's Seventh; and on the morning of the Sunday of the final concert I went up to Riverdale to speak to Walter Toscanini about something. His father had already moved to the other house; and while I was talking to Walter in the large living room off the central hall, the door opened and Mme. Toscanini, in a dressing gown, looked in but withdrew hastily when she saw me. Shortly afterward the door opened again; and this time it was Toscanini, in slippers and a brocaded silk dressing gown over his undershirt and trousers, and with the small score of Haydn's No. 99 in his hand. "You can see," he said, opening the score to the beginning of the first movement after the slow introduction, and pointing, "is writ-

ten Vivace assai; but X—— play too slow. Is dilettante!" And
from this excessively slow tempo he went on to others, of
which I now remember only one—that of Pamina's "Ach, ich
fühl's" in The Magic Flute. Clasping his hands as he acted
Pamina's agitation, he exclaimed: "Pamina say 'I lose my
Tamino! Where my Tamino!' Must be Andante, but is always
Adagio!"

"Senti,"[4] said Walter at one point, taking out a handker-
chief and patting his father's face with it. "Why are you
perspiring?"

"Because I am warm!" Toscanini answered vehemently.
"When I talk about music I am not cold!"

A little later Walter told him that the master of the first
side of the 1936 recording of Beethoven's Seventh couldn't
be used any longer, and Victor asked him to listen to a pressing from the master of one of his other "takes" of that side.
As Walter was putting the record on the turntable Toscanini
said to me: "I never like first side. Is too slow." And when
the sound of the suggested replacement began to emerge from
the speaker his face lighted up and he exclaimed: "So is correct!" Astonished by all this, I asked: "But who chose the
old side?" Toscanini apparently didn't hear me; and it was
Walter who, standing behind his father, pointed at him with
a grin. Only later did I remember Toscanini's statement in
Philadelphia that the 1936 recordings had been passed on by
a committee of Gilman, Betti and Chotzinoff; which meant
that Walter was mistaken.

Eventually Toscanini left the room; and when I had finished talking with Walter and was about to leave, his father
reappeared, dressed for the day, and invited me upstairs to
see the three picture views that were framed by the three win-
dows of his study. We went out onto the terrace; and some
point connected with his imminent NBC broadcast of Gershwin's Rhapsody in Blue came up that caused him to speak
with sorrow about Gershwin who had been "very simpatico."

Toscanini also conducted the Philharmonic in a Red Cross

4 "Listen."

concert devoted to Wagner, late in November, with Traubel again as soloist in the *Tristan* and *Götterdämmerung* finales. I remember him, at the beginning of the first rehearsal, working patiently to achieve the accuracy, the balance, the radiance of the opening chords of the *Lohengrin* Prelude; and I remember him, at the end of the last rehearsal, in a rage about something the orchestra hadn't done as he wished in the *Götterdämmerung* finale. When this rehearsal was over, Walter invited me to visit his father in his dressing room, where I expected to find him still raging—instead of which I found him seated on a sofa, his powerful torso bare, the sweat dripping off the tip of his nose, and a look of pleasure on his face as he searched eagerly in the full score of *Die Götterdämmerung* open in his lap. "I am sure," he exclaimed, "Brünnhilde is very unhappy. . . . Yes"—having found what he was looking for, and pointing to it—" '*Verraten*'!⁵ She is '*verraten*'!" And reading further: "Yes . . . '*Alles, Alles weiss ich*.'⁶ Yes. . . ."

Shortly before this he conducted the Philadelphia Orchestra in Mozart's G-minor, the Overture and Bacchanale of Wagner's *Tannhäuser*, and the Musorgsky-Ravel *Pictures at an Exhibition*. I heard the repetition of the concert in New York on November 24, and was surprised by the change in my feeling about the performance of the G-minor. It had always impressed me as too impassioned, and to the performance issued in Victor M-631 in 1939 I had even applied the terms 'tumultuous' and 'ferocious'; but the performance with the Philadelphia Orchestra I now found to be completely and satisfyingly right; and when I went back to the 1939 Victor recording and also to an off-the-air recording of the last Philharmonic performance in 1936, I was astonished to hear the same tempos and the same powerful phrasing and shaping. It was clearly I who had changed (and I discovered this to be true also when I went back to the Beecham performance of the symphony in Columbia M-316, which I had previously considered excellent, and was shocked now by the inappropriate jauntiness of the opening statements—especially the effect of the sharp clipping off of their conclusions—and by the

⁵ "Betrayed."
⁶ "All, all do I understand."

expressive inadequacy of the treatment of the entire first movement).

But on the other hand, listening at this time to the performances of Brahms's symphonies in an NBC Brahms cycle, I knew that in some instances Toscanini had changed in the course of years. Remembering clearly the swift and light-footed progression of the first movement of the Third when he had first played it here in 1929, I was struck by the breadth and weight of the performance now; and there was a similar change in the first movement of the Fourth. These were the first such changes I was aware of in Toscanini's performances; but others as striking, and more significant, were to reveal themselves a couple of years later.

The Brahms cycle included the *German Requiem*; and before the final rehearsal there was the pre-rehearsal hubbub of the orchestra tuning and practicing and the Westminster Choir warming up on syllables like "mi-mi-mi-mi"—to all of which Toscanini seemed oblivious as he talked animatedly with Samuel Chotzinoff, pointing now in this direction at the stage and now in that. At last Toscanini finished with Chotzinoff and went up onto the stage to begin the rehearsal; and it had proceeded for some time when, in a rage at some failure of the chorus, he shouted: "Is not enough to sing 'mi-mi-mi-mi-mi'!" Evidently he was oblivious to no sound.

Several other NBC Symphony performances and rehearsals of that season remain in my memory. The Verdi program of January 31, 1943, offered the exciting experiences of performances which revealed the dramatic power, eloquence and nobility of the early music from *Nabucco* and *I Lombardi* as well as the more familiar *La Forza del Destino* and *La Traviata*. The first rehearsal was unprecedentedly late in starting, with the concertmaster Mischakoff's chair conspicuously vacant. At last Mischakoff appeared, followed by Toscanini; and the reason for the delay became evident when Toscanini began to conduct the long instrumental introduction to the Trio from *I Lombardi*, of which the violin solo was played by Mischakoff in an Italian-opera vocal style that he hadn't learned in the conservatory in his youth.

Another Verdi program on July 25 offered the additional

exciting experiences of hearing familiar matters like "*O don fatale*" from *Don Carlo*, "*Pace, pace, mio Dio*" from *La Forza del Destino*, "*Eri tu*" from *Un Ballo in Maschera*, and the entire fourth act of *Rigoletto* emerge "as fresh and glistening as creation itself" in performances in which every detail of the accurately and beautifully played orchestral part was in active expressive relation to what was being sung; the accurately and expressively shaped vocal phrases fitted precisely into the orchestral contexts; and the progression of integrated vocal and orchestral parts was clear in outline and texture, coherent in shape, continuous in tension. (The *Rigoletto* act—with Jan Peerce, Gertrude Ribla, Nan Merriman, Francesco Valentino and Nicola Moscona—was Toscanini's first performance of opera in New York since 1915; and he repeated it—with Zinka Milanov and Leonard Warren in place of Ribla and Valentino—at his Red Cross concert in Madison Square Garden on May 25, 1944.)

The same impression of the familiar pieces being revealed as though newly created was produced at the rehearsal of Tchaikovsky's *Nutcracker Suite* for a Carnegie Hall concert on April 25, and at the rehearsals of a program of "pop" numbers broadcast on April 4. The members of the orchestra sat smiling in pleasure at the phrasing and pacing of the Overture to *Zampa*, the best-known Boccherini Minuet, the *Dance of the Hours*, Liszt's Second Hungarian Rhapsody, *The Stars and Stripes Forever*; and they applauded the exquisite inflection of the long melody of the Haydn Serenade from the Quartet Op. 3 No. 5.

This, I believe, was the first of such programs of "pop" numbers, which must have impressed less sophisticated listeners as well as the members of the NBC Symphony and myself. That is, it seemed to me that a musically unsophisticated person, listening to these pieces that he knew well, would inevitably be struck by the things that were different about them this time—that listening, for example, to *The Stars and Stripes Forever* he would notice not only the general liveliness and buoyancy but the subordinate melodies or accompanying figures that he had never before heard so clearly outlined and so beautifully modeled; and that in this way he might get an idea of the differences that were possible in performances, and of the particular qualities of Toscanini's performances, which previously he might have thought people only pretended they heard.

At a rehearsal for the June 20 broadcast of lighter classics the tempo of the first part of Debussy's *Prélude à L'Après-midi d'un faune* was strikingly faster than that of other conductors' performances; and happening to be following with the score I discovered what was behind it. Debussy's direction for the tempo of the first part was "Very moderate"; for the middle part it was "First rate of movement"; for the return of the first part it was "Movement of the beginning"; and whereas the usual practice was to play the first part more slowly than the rest, Toscanini obeyed Debussy's directions to maintain the one pace throughout by bringing the first part up to the tempo of the rest. (Years earlier, when he had first played Brahms's First Symphony in New York, he had similarly decided that the Poco sostenuto of the introduction to the first movement must be the same as the Poco sostenuto of the similar passage at the end of the movement. This turned out to be too fast for the proper effect of the introduction; nevertheless in all the three or four performances of the symphony that year Toscanini stuck to this consistency at the cost of effectiveness; but when he played the work again in a later season he took the introduction to the first movement at its traditionally slower pace.)

And there were, finally, the rehearsals of *La Mer* for the broadcast of April 11. At the first, Toscanini worked on the detail of the first two movements; then, finding himself with only a few minutes left, he led the orchestra straight through the final movement in a breathtakingly beautiful and effective performance that caused the orchestra to applaud him at the end. The next day he perfected the detail of this movement and then went through the entire work in a way that impelled the orchestra, at the end, to burst into a storm of applause in appreciation of the imaginative insight and technical powers that had integrated all the bits of color and figuration and all the nuances of tempo into the coherent and magnificent form in sound. It was on this occasion that the young violinist exclaimed to me: "You can quote me on this: we come here to go to school!"

On February 6, 1944, Toscanini conducted the Philadelphia Orchestra in a Pension Fund concert; and I went to Philadelphia for the last two rehearsals. The Beethoven program comprised the *Egmont* Overture, the Septet, the *Pastoral* Symphony and the *Leonore* No. 2 Overture; and at the first of the rehearsals, at which the symphony was worked on, I was bowled over by what the phrasing of the orchestra's great solo flute, William Kincaid, and solo oboe, Marcel Tabuteau, made of the passage of bird calls at the end of the second movement. ("Well," a New York musician replied when I spoke of this, "after all, they've been doing it together for twenty-five years.") The performance of the symphony seemed very fine to me; but after the rehearsal a member of the orchestra whom I knew remarked: "I'm a little surprised at the things he's letting pass," referring to details of execution which an orchestra player's ear would notice but other listeners' would not.

At the final rehearsal the next morning, after a little more work on parts of the symphony, the *Leonore* No. 2 was done; then came the break, and as some of the men started to leave the stage Tabuteau called them back. Turning to Toscanini, he told him of the pleasure it had been for the orchestra to play with him, of its gratitude for his coming to conduct this concert—in token of which it presented him with this scroll; and he handed it to Toscanini who at once, in childlike curiosity, unrolled it and began to read it as Tabuteau continued to speak. Then Toscanini spoke briefly but warmly in reply, ending with the statement that nothing in the future could be certain but "consider me always at your disposition," which the orchestra applauded. And then he went to his dressing room, while the men who weren't needed for the rehearsal of the Septet packed up their instruments and left.

It was therefore in a very happy atmosphere that the rehearsal of the Septet began after the break, with young Samuel Mayes, the first cellist, swaying happily from side to side as he sawed away on his instrument in the Minuet. But suddenly the sky clouded: in the variation movement a fast passage for the violins was repeated but did not satisfy Toscanini; it was repeated again and still did not satisfy him; he called now on one or two desks of the first violins ("You! you! I hear you!") to repeat it; and then the storm broke. It became evident that he was raging not just about what had gone wrong in the Septet but about all the things he had let pass in the symphony; as for the passage in the Septet, "I play this piece with NBC," he shouted at the violins, "and you are not so wonderful!—no!—you are not so wonderful!—no!—NO!" —a shockingly cruel thing to say to a group which actually *was* very wonderful (its playing in the *Pastoral* had a beauty and finish which the NBC Symphony's did not have in a performance a few weeks later) and which, in the years since Stokowski's departure, had been fighting with gallantry and success to maintain itself as the great orchestra he had made it. The men sat in impassive silence until Toscanini's anger had spent itself and he resumed the rehearsal. At the end of the piece he remained standing on the podium, silent, motionless, brooding; and suddenly Tabuteau was at his side, with an arm affectionately on his shoulder, asking him if he would like another rehearsal of the strings just before the concert that evening. Toscanini brightened: Yes, he would like it; the players nodded their heads vigorously in agreement. And so the rehearsal ended.

I am sure Tabuteau's gesture of affection was genuine. It is my impression that intelligent orchestra players didn't regard Toscanini's rages as mere self-indulgence by a man who could be reasonable and patient but felt privileged to be unreasonable and impatient. I think they understood that he was, in his relation to music, a man obsessed and possessed, and that such a man was not rational and reasonable—not in music nor in anything else; and some of them may have perceived what that remarkably perceptive critic, W. J. Turner, spoke of in a review of Toscanini's concerts in London in 1935. As he had sat watching Toscanini, Turner had been "suddenly reminded of Berlioz's remark, 'Do you think I make music for my pleasure?' I am certain that it is not a pleasure for Toscanini to conduct, but rather that he suffers. It is because of his extreme musical sensibility and intense concentration. Here lies the essence of his superiority." I thought this perception of Toscanini's suffering true even before Toscanini confirmed it in a statement years later. Not self-indulgence, then, but extreme musical sensibility, intense concentration, suffering—these were some of the causes of the rages: "Put your blood!" he roared once at a rehearsal of an insignificant little Italian piece. "*I* put *my* blood!" And they were reasons for intelligent orchestra players to forgive him, as they did.

Late in October 1944 I wrote Toscanini that I was having a copy of my new book, *Music for the Man Who Enjoys "Hamlet,"* sent to him; and that I had thought he wouldn't care for a published dedication, but wanted him to know the book was dedicated to him privately in acknowledgment of my debt to him. To this I received a reply dated November 3, in which he said that I had guessed his feeling correctly—that the dedication of the book on its front page would not have been as dear to him as it was now that it came silently from my mind and heart; and from the bottom of his heart came his best thanks. As for my statement about acknowledgment of my debt to him, he said it made him blush, as he had blushed that day when he had listened to the recording of the *Eroica* that had been made a few years ago. Then he asked when he would have the pleasure of seeing me in Riverdale. He hoped it would be soon—possibly the next week: he wanted very badly to ask me something about my book. And he ended with best good wishes and very cordially.

The recording of Beethoven's *Eroica* he referred to was Victor M-765, which had been made during a broadcast in November 1939; and he had listened to it in preparation for the performance he broadcast on November 5, 1944. The recorded sound of the 1939 performance was the unresonantly dry, flat, hard, tight sound of Studio 8H filled with an audience; the performance itself was one of his greatest. But it was a performance in his earlier expansive style marked by great elasticity of tempo—one which, for rhetorical emphasis, paused for an instant after each of the two forceful chords that claim attention at the beginning of the first movement of the *Eroica*, and which, in the subsequent course of the movement, slowed down momentarily to introduce a new section or broadened out for a climax. And the performance of November 5, 1944, was a striking illustration of the important change in Toscanini's style since 1939—the change away from the expansiveness and toward a swifter, tauter, subtler simplicity involving only slight modification of the set tempo.[7] But for Toscanini the change was not just a change from one way of playing to another: it was a change to a right way, to the only right way, and from a way, therefore, that had been shamefully wrong. (I might suggest in passing that this habit of mind, rather than the jealousy he was accused of, was responsible for some of his unfavorable estimates of other conductors. His intense conviction at a particular moment that *this* was the right way to conduct a phrase or a movement made all other ways—his own in the past, another conductor's now—appear to him shamefully wrong.)

As for the tendency to swifter, tauter simplicity, it was not without exceptions in the reverse direction: the 1939 Beethoven cycle that included the expansive *Eroica* also included a Ninth whose first movement was faster and less expansive than the first movement in the February 1938 performance; but the first movement of the Ninth recorded in 1952 was slower, and at certain climactic points more powerfully expansive, than the one of 1939; and the *Tristan* Prelude and Finale recorded in 1952 also was enormously slower and more powerfully expansive than the one of 1942. I might add that on occasion the swifter tautness was carried to the point of

[7] Let me make it clear that this later simplification of style was something different from the setting of a single tempo for an entire movement, which I spoke of on page 16. In both the 1939 and the 1944 performances Toscanini set a single tempo for the first movement and again for the second; but in the earlier performance the modifications of the set tempo were expansive, whereas in the later one they were subtle. And I might add that of two performances in the same tempo, one—because of the particular state of Toscanini's mind and emotions at the moment—might exhibit strikingly more or strikingly less power than the other, or might exhibit a tenseness and rigidity which the other did not.

excessively fast rigidity—as in the Haydn *Surprise* Symphony recorded in 1953; but to this I would have to add that within a week or two of the Haydn performance Toscanini recorded the relaxed performances of Schubert's C-major, Dvořák's *New World* and Rossini's Overture to *William Tell*. Also, the earlier slower and more expansive performance often was more effective than the later faster and simpler one; but not always: the *Eroicas* of November 1944, February 1949, and December 1953 had hair-raising power in their simpler style. And it is interesting that the Scherzo of Mendelssohn's Octet recorded in 1945 was at once faster, more relaxed, and more brilliantly effective than the one in the 1947 broadcast performance issued on Victor LM-1869.

I wrote to Toscanini that it would be a great pleasure to visit him whenever he had time; and a few days after the *Eroica* broadcast I received a note apologizing for the delay—he had been very busy—and suggesting that I come up the following afternoon. When I arrived I found him—ruddy, bright-eyed, genial, his after-lunch toothpick still in his mouth —sitting in a sunny corner of the living room with Mme. Toscanini, who was sewing or crocheting. He rose to welcome me as Mme. Toscanini smiled her greeting; then he led me to an easy chair, sat down on the sofa next to it, and leaned forward to slap my knee as he exclaimed with a smile: "Always fighting!"

Then, "I want to ask you a question about your book. I am stupid in such things. How do you use instrument for measuring?" He was referring to the little cardboard ruler that had been provided with the book to measure places on phonograph records where details I mentioned could be heard. And it was true—as the scratched records and damaged styli testified—that he was very awkward in his dealings with records. We went to the phonograph, and I showed him how I used the ruler to find a place on one of the Victor *Eroica* records. "Is there much difference in records?" he asked; and I showed him in the book the differences in the measurements of the several recordings of the *Eroica*. "And you did all this work!" he exclaimed. "It must be much time." And apparently the measuring procedure still seemed formidable to him, for he said: "I will ask my son; I am stupid in such things."

His mind now reverted to the preceding Sunday's perform-ance of the *Eroica*; and he went to the piano. "I listen to record: the first *accords* are still played with pauses. Sunday for the first time I have courage to play in tempo—so:" and he played the two opening chords in strict tempo. And con-cerning this tempo: "Forty years ago when I play *Eroica* the first time I hear German conductors—I hear Richter—and I think I must play this German music as they play it—so:" and he demonstrated their slow tempo in the first movement. "But when I play this symphony later I play more and more as I feel; and now I have courage at last to take right tempo— so:" and he demonstrated his tempo of the preceding Sunday, characterizing it, as he played, as "easy . . . easy . . ." "Also in second movement: always I am afraid and play bass part first two times so:" and he played the first appoggiatura note on the beat. "Why—when Beethoven write third time so:" and he played the appoggiatura notes in advance of the beat. "Now I tell *bassi*: 'Play first times so:'" and he played the appog-giatura notes in advance of the beat. "Because Beethoven is very exact—but even Beethoven sometimes write different"; and he cited the pizzicato note that Beethoven wrote now as an eighth-note, now as a quarter, now as a half.

"Germans play everything too slow," he said. The second movement of Beethoven's Seventh, for example: "I have cour-age to play so:" and he demonstrated his faster-than-usual Al-legretto. "Rodzinski play so:" and he demonstrated the slower tempo. "I asked him: 'My dear, why you do this?' He say: 'Is *marcia funebre*.' I say: 'No, is not *marcia funebre*; is so:'" and he demonstrated. "But he play again the same way."

The slow movement of Beethoven's Second was another ex-ample; after which Toscanini commented: "Beethoven write only one Adagio—in Ninth Symphony. He put metronome mark 60—3—no, 60; for second part he put 63. Is not much difference; *allóra*[8] I make so—and so:" and he demonstrated the two tempos of the alternating sections. "But Furtwängler

8 then

make so:" and he demonstrated Furtwängler's slower tempos. In Mozart also 2/4 was converted into 4/8, Andante into Adagio. "All German conductors play Mozart Andante too slow"; and he illustrated first with the Andante of the Symphony in E flat, then with the Andante of the *Jupiter*, playing the latter first as an Adagio with dragging accompaniment eighths, then as a flowing Andante. Concerning the G-minor he had a different complaint: "When I hear G-minor from German conductors the first time, was so:" and he played a jauntily phrased statement of the opening theme of the first movement. But with the Overture to *Don Giovanni* it was again "Always Mozart is too slow": the introduction of the overture should be in the same tempo as when it accompanied the Commendatore's singing at the end of the opera. And there was a difference between the 2/4 time of *Don Giovanni* and the 2/4 of *The Magic Flute*: the right tempo for *Là ci darem la mano* was too slow for Papageno's aria. "When I conduct *Flauto Magico* in Salzburg I am afraid about my tempi; but Rosé [the old concertmaster of the Vienna State Opera Orchestra] say once 'At last!' I tell Bruno Walter 'You will not like my tempi in *Flauto Magico*.' He say 'Is very interesting'; but afterward he make again slow tempi. . . . All German conductors play too slow! Muck! Was terrible! *Orchestra* [the Boston Symphony] was wonderful. But he make program: Haydn Symphony in *re*—the last [No. 104], Mozart [Jupiter?] and Beethoven [First?]; and everything so *slow!* Muck was Beckmesser of conductors!"

I think it was somewhere in all this that Toscanini referred to the excessively slow tempo not of a conductor but of a pianist. "When Serkin play with me Mozart Concerto in B flat [K.595, which Serkin performed with the New York Philharmonic in 1936] I say I know Schnabel's slow tempo in Larghetto, but I am sure this music should be *alla breve*. And once Serkin send me from Europe photograph of Mozart manuscript of Larghetto: is written *alla breve!*"

Something reminded him of what he had been reading about Wagner's conducting. "You know this life of Wagner by—by—by——" He couldn't remember the name, and went to get the book, which turned out to be the W. Ashton Ellis biography. "You have not read this? Ee-e-e! It describe Wagner's conducting in London . . . is very interesting. Wagner make something which I cannot imagine: Largo in *passage* [the French word] in first movement of *Jupiter* Symphony; but where? Slow movement he play without *sordini* . . . he must play slow movement like Germans—too slow. He make big ritard in last part of Minuet; but where? Is clear, Wagner conduct *a piacere*;[9] but I cannot imagine what they say he do." And he insisted on my taking the book to read.

Before I left I inscribed his copy of my book with "To Arturo Toscanini" and my signature. And a few weeks later I received his Christmas card, which he had inscribed in similar fashion to me. The printed portion of the card had on one page a photograph of Toscanini looking at a framed picture of Beethoven in his hand, and underneath the first measures of the Andante maestoso section in the finale of the Ninth, with the words *Seid umschlungen, Millionen! Diesen Kuss der ganzen Welt!*, copied out by Toscanini; and on the opposite page his handwritten Christmas and New Year greeting and signature.

The *Eroica* of November 5, 1944, was part of a Beethoven cycle which included the Piano Concertos Nos. 1, 3 and 4, and which was brought to an especially notable conclusion with a performance of *Fidelio*. Toscanini didn't often play concertos, and this because of his way of regarding and treating them. A Beethoven or Mozart concerto usually is not something which a conductor puts on a program for itself, and for which he then engages a suitable pianist. It is, rather, something he has to play for a soloist who has been engaged for his box-office drawing power, and something the conductor has little interest in, since its purpose is to show off the soloist, not himself. As a result the performance usually is the product of only enough rehearsal—sometimes a mere single run-through—for the soloist's and orchestra's playing to be geared together in time. A concerto performance in which the orchestral part has been carefully worked out is rare; and rarest of all is the kind of performance Schnabel insisted on—in which

9 with freedom

the solo and orchestral parts were integrated in every detail of phrasing and style (mostly *his* phrasing and style). Now there were exceptional instances in which Toscanini too began with the soloist—one being Myra Hess's appearance with the NBC Symphony in November 1946, which was his salute to her in recognition of her war work. But in most instances he began with the concerto; and in all instances he treated it as something worth playing for itself: listening to the performance one heard a carefully rehearsed orchestral part in which familiar phrases acquired amazingly new contours and significance, and counterpoints and figurations previously unheard in the mass of sound emerged with startling clarity and impact from the newly transparent textures; and one heard all these things related in a continuous progression which was built up into a coherent and powerful structure. It was an exciting experience; and it remained that even when the structure was built up around nothing—i.e., the characterless flow of sounds produced by Ania Dorfman in Beethoven's Piano Concerto No. 1. Or around something as alien in style as Artur Rubinstein's playing in No. 3. I still remember the occasion when Iturbi, in performances of Mozart's Concertos K.466 and 467 with Toscanini and the New York Philharmonic, was impelled by the orchestra's powerfully phrased playing to match it with a strong inflection of phrase that was in striking contrast to his usual salon-music style in Mozart. But the hair-raising power of the orchestral part of Beethoven's No. 3 had no such effect on Rubinstein, who played with his usual on-the-surface brilliance and elegance, and gave the florid melodic passages in the slow movement Chopinesque inflections. Only Serkin's playing in No. 4—though often unimpressive in its mere fluency, in comparison with Schnabel's strongly inflected playing—had the right over-all character and sufficient vitality to fit well into Toscanini's orchestral framework.

We come, then, to the matter of Toscanini's strange choices of soloists—strange in view of the reason he once gave me for playing concertos infrequently: that he could not operate as a mere accompanist, but had to be satisfied with the soloist's playing of *his* part. In illustration he cited the case of Ossip Gabrilowitsch. In 1935 Toscanini conducted a Brahms cycle in which Gabrilowitsch was announced as the soloist in the Piano Concerto No. 2, a famous specialty of his. A few weeks before the date of the performance I was surprised to see Toscanini sitting in front of me at a concert at which Gabrilowitsch played the same Brahms concerto with the National Orchestral Association; subsequently the Philharmonic announced the cancellation of the work because of Gabrilowitsch's illness; and now Toscanini confirmed my suspicion that he had canceled the work because he hadn't been able to accept Gabrilowitsch's way of playing it. Yet he *had* been able to accept Rubinstein's way of playing the Beethoven No. 3. Nor was this the only instance. His own taste had been evident in the delicacy and purity of Remo Bolognini's style in a marvelously light and winged Philharmonic performance of Mendelssohn's Violin Concerto in the thirties; yet in a performance of this work in the spring of 1944 he had accepted the pretentiously mannered and sentimentally distorted phrasing of Heifetz. He was fanatical about setting the right tempo, about maintaining it once it was set; and his strong convictions about this made him inflexible; yet he accepted Myra Hess's slowing down of the first movement of Beethoven's No. 3 after the orchestral introduction, and a slower tempo in the second movement than he had taken in the performance with Rubinstein. Clearly, Toscanini exhibited most of the time a taste, in the exercise of which he was rigorous and unyielding; but there was occasional inconsistency in the taste itself, and occasional yielding in its exercise. If I am correct in my impression that Rubinstein was not one of the close friends, his case illustrates inconsistency in the taste itself; but the cases of friends like Dorfman and Heifetz, and of Horowitz, who was married to Toscanini's daughter Wanda (and whose mannered phrasing one would have expected Toscanini not to like) appear to demonstrate that Toscanini's taste could be by-passed by way of his heart. And with Hess his convictions seem to have yielded to her war record.

So with *Fidelio*. Nobody could fuss more than Toscanini did about getting the exactly right singer for a part in an opera; but the Leonore of the broadcast *Fidelio* was Rose Bampton, whose monotonously shrill upper range was not exactly right for this part, and who marred the performance by breaking on the final high note of *Komm' Hoffnung* (a later recording of the aria was substituted in Victor LM-6025), but who was a close friend of the Toscanini family. And I must assume that someone put in an influential word for another singer whose badly accented German made him grossly unfit for his participation in the performance.

What it comes to is that Toscanini, aside from being a great musician, was a human being with the inconsistencies and contradictions—which is to say with the fallibilities and weaknesses—of any other human being. This is hardly surprising; but people who expect, understand and accept the fallibilities and weaknesses in a businessman or an engineer were surprised—and even shocked and outraged—by them in Toscanini, believing apparently that a man who was as great an artist as he must be perfect in all other respects. But I contend that in addition to the reasons for the Toscaninis of this world to behave no better than the businessmen and engineers, there are reasons for them to behave even worse. Not only are their traits of personality and character, like those of businessmen and engineers, conditioned, developed and distorted by the ordinary experiences with family, friends, enemies, teachers, employers; but their lives are subjected to the additional distorting strains of their intensive training and their careers; and sometimes they begin with the unbalance that makes possible a fanatical dedication and concentration during long years of training and then during the years of artistic achievement. If Toscanini had not been, in relation to music, a man obsessed and possessed, willing to endure the suffering caused by his extreme musical sensibility and concentration, he would not have s bjected people to the unreasonable, inconsiderate, bad-tempered, sometimes downright cruel behavior described in Chotzinoff's *Toscanini: An Intimate Portrait*; but we would not have had his performances. And having had the performances, we owe him not only gratitude for the experiences he gave us and for his willingness to endure what made those experiences possible, but the same understanding and tolerance of his behavior as we give the businessman and the engineer.

It may have occurred to some to wonder why Rubinstein and why not Schnabel? Toscanini did speak of Schnabel—not on the occasion when he explained his not playing concertos, but on another. Sitting at the piano, he said: "I must ask you —I do not understand why you write so about Schnabel. In Beethoven G-major Concerto [I had written about the piano's opening statement being made by Schnabel 'quietly, deeply, spaciously meditative'] he play so:" and Toscanini astonished me by playing the piano's opening statement with gross distentions that hadn't the slightest resemblance to Schnabel's subtle inflection. "And in Schubert *Moment musical* [I had written that Schnabel played these pieces 'with wonderful feeling for their delicacy and subtlety'] he play so:" and Toscanini astonished me again by playing the best-known F-minor with similar gross distentions that hadn't the slightest resemblance to Schnabel's enchantingly simple and graceful treatment of it. Clearly there was a personal antipathy which impelled Toscanini's ear to hear incorrectly the objective facts of Schnabel's performances. And the antipathy was mutual: "He thinks only *he* is pure!" Schnabel once exclaimed to me scornfully. "I know: I traveled with him one night in the train to Milan."

On January 13, 1945, Toscanini conducted the New York Philharmonic in a Pension Fund concert, repeating the program of his first concert with the orchestra on January 14, 1926: Haydn's Symphony No. 101 (*Clock*), Respighi's *Pines of Rome*, Sibelius's *Swan of Tuonela*, *Siegfried's Death and Funeral Music* from Wagner's *Götterdämmerung*, and Weber's Overture to *Euryanthe*. He had repeated the program also at his final Thursday-Friday pair in April 1936; and it looked as if this was a second and final farewell to the orchestra, which he signalized by writing out the program for facsimile reproduction in the program notes. Far from exhibiting any diminution of his powers, the performances seemed to be the ones of 1926 and 1936 with their wonderful qualities heightened; and this impression was confirmed a few years later when I heard a private recording of the concert and compared the Haydn *Clock* Symphony with the 1929 performance in Victor M-57:

the later one was made even more dazzling by the faster tempo, greater energy and sharper inflection.

And again the bond between Toscanini and the orchestra was demonstrated at the first rehearsal—this time in even more impressive fashion than in 1942. Then he had returned to an orchestra only slightly changed in personnel and not at all disciplined by another conductor; now he returned to an orchestra in which Rodzinski had made a considerable number of replacements and which he had drilled for two years. Nevertheless, having first devoted a few minutes to working out the cross-rhythm at the climax of the Wagner piece and the balance of the wind instruments in the opening chords, Toscanini then simply led the orchestra through it without interruption and produced every sound and contour of the performance of 1936—as though there had been no interval of nine years, no changes in personnel, no other conductor. It was, as in 1942, his way of saying: "This is *my* orchestra."

Nor did I hear any diminution of his powers in the performances of Weber's Overture to *Der Freischütz*, Ravel's *La Valse* and the Musorgsky-Ravel *Pictures at an Exhibition* at a benefit concert with the NBC Symphony (there was also the Brahms B-flat Concerto with Horowitz, which I didn't hear). But when I visited him shortly afterward he asked how the performances had sounded, and then told me he had been ill and fearful of not getting through the concert, and had conducted *Pictures* with no knowledge and control of what he was doing.

At this visit his mind was full of Haydn's Symphony No. 98, which he had played during his first NBC season and was preparing to play again. The preparation, as usual, consisted in studying the score, listening to the recording of the 1938 broadcast, and reading what he had found in print about the work—Tovey's comments in *Essays in Musical Analysis*. Mentioning Tovey's demonstration of the remarkable similarity between a passage in the slow movement and a passage in the Andante of Mozart's *Jupiter*, Toscanini went on to say, to my amazement, that he considered Haydn greater than Mozart. "I will tell you frankly: sometimes I find Mozart boring. Not G-minor: that is great tragedy; and not concerti; but other

music. Is always beautiful—but is always the same." And what
he had in mind became clear when he played the record of
the 1938 broadcast of Haydn's No. 98: he sat conducting the
performance, signaling to me when something was about to
happen, smiling his delight when it happened; and it was evident that what delighted him was Haydn's liveliness of mind—
the surprises he contrived for his listeners in melody, harmony,
rhythm, orchestration. Above all orchestration: it was also evident that as a conductor Toscanini was delighted most by the
variety, freshness and ingenuity of Haydn's use of the orchestra—details like the one Toscanini pointed to in the Minuet,
exclaiming gleefully: "Flutes and basses!" Nor was it only
Haydn who surpassed Mozart in this respect, he said, but also
Rossini—as he undertook to show me with the orchestral ingenuity and variety of the Overture to *La Cenerentola*. And
here something characteristic happened: putting on the turntable what he thought was the record with the *Cenerentola*
performance, he stood listening with surprise as the scherzo
movement of Tchaikovsky's *Manfred* came out of the speaker
instead; then, his hands involuntarily beginning to move with
the music, he gradually became completely involved with it
and conducted it to the end of the record—after which he remembered *La Cenerentola*, found the correct record, and conducted that, pointing out to me the orchestral details that
delighted him.

The performance of Haydn's No. 98 that Toscanini broadcast on March 25, 1945, and recorded afterward was, and is,
superb considered by itself: only when one compared it with
the 1938 performance did one discover that it was less expansive and relaxed, and as a result less effective. Similarly
the V-J Day performance of Beethoven's *Eroica*, characteristic and impressive by itself, revealed—when compared with
the 1944 and 1939 performances—a shocking lessened energy.
And the possibility that Toscanini's powers might be failing
was raised by the performances in his regular NBC series the
following winter—performances whose extreme rigidity suggested the alarming possibility of a change in his mental proc-
esses analogous to the stiffening of the movements of an aging

body. I recall in particular a driving, tense first movement of Brahms's Fourth that was in shocking contrast to the slower, relaxed, expansive one three years before; and a Mozart G-minor without the fluidity and energy of the 1939 performance in Victor M-631.

It was not until the fall of 1946 that a lessening of the rigidity, tenseness and drive and a return of relaxed plasticity began to manifest themselves—most notably and excitingly in the November 3 performance of Mozart's Divertimento K.287 for horns and strings. It was on another occasion that Toscanini remarked to me how difficult it was to play Mozart—how boring the music could be unless one knew what to do between the *p* here and the *f* eight measures later; but the comment was relevant to this performance of the Divertimento, which not only had the old fluidity and grace, but revealed Toscanini's knowledge of what to do between the *p*'s and *f*'s in the profusion of subtle inflection that delightfully enlivened the Allegros, gave exquisite contours to the variation movement, and shaped the Adagio as a grandly impassioned vocal declamation with a cumulative expressive force that was breathtaking. And the broadcast also offered a performance of Mozart's *Haffner* Symphony which—in contrast to the expansively plastic 1929 performance in Victor M-65—exhibited a simplification and clarification that made it grand and apotheosized.

I wrote enthusiastically to Toscanini about the Divertimento performance; and when, shortly afterward, I went up to the Villa Pauline to visit him, he met me at the door of his study with the pocket score of the Divertimento in his hand. "I will tell you why I play this piece," he said. "I listen last summer to Tanglewood—" and he shook his head and rolled his eyes heavenward at the memory of what he had heard. Opening the score and pointing to the bass part, he said: "Koussevitzky use *celli* without *bassi; allóra* sometimes violas play lower than bass part." Also, Koussevitzky's tempo in the variation movement had been too slow for the prescribed Andante and for the character of the music. But most shocking of all had been what happened near the end of the Adagio, where Toscanini showed me in the score the usual indication, which any musician would understand, for the interpolation of a cadenza: the halt on an anticipatory six-four chord, followed by a rest for the interpolated cadenza, and a trill to conclude the cadenza and bring in the orchestra for the rest of the movement. And Toscanini's face now expressed the horror with which he had heard the Boston Symphony pause on the six-four chord, break off for the rest, and—without any cadenza having been interpolated—play the trill and conclude the movement. "This man is no musician!" Toscanini exclaimed. "Is *ignorante!*" He had therefore played the Divertimento correctly for Koussevitzky's instruction: "I think maybe he listen."

Walter Toscanini, who meanwhile had been searching among the 16-inch acetate recordings of the NBC broadcasts, now had what he had been looking for—the recording of the November 3 broadcast of the Divertimento. As he put it on the turntable his father seated me at his desk with the score open before me; and standing behind me and looking over my shoulder he conducted the entire performance as it came out of the speaker. At one point in the first movement where the first violins swept up to a series of high A's he chuckled and exclaimed: "Is difficult!"; and when later in the movement they swept up to an analogous series of high B-flats he again chuckled and exclaimed: "Is difficult!"[10]

---

[10] By the time the Divertimento episode got into Howard Taubman's book, *The Maestro*, it had been transformed as follows: "On another occasion he confided that he had made a recording of Mozart's Divertimento for strings and two horns for the benefit of his colleagues, the conductors. . . . In the slow movement he had always felt something lacking and decided what was needed was a cadenza for the first violin. After he had made this addition, Toscanini found a letter from Mozart to his wife which confirmed his hunch." The letter is not to be found in the Mozart correspondence, and a cadenza, by its very nature, is not something of which the need is suspected. And reviewing the book in *The Nation* I pointed out that this incident didn't belong with the stories about Toscanini puzzling over something in a score and reaching a conclusion about it that was confirmed later by documentary evidence; that in this instance, on the contrary, the entire point had been the score's explicit indication of the cadenza by the six-four chord, rest and trill, which Koussevitzky had not heeded, causing Toscanini to pronounce him *ignorante*.

In the time since the 1944 *Fidelio* Toscanini had broadcast the opening scene of Bellini's *Norma* and the Prologue of Boito's *Mefistofele* in December 1945, and all of Puccini's *La Bohème* in March 1946. And on December 1 and 8 of that year he broadcast Verdi's *La Traviata*. Only a few days before the first half Carl Van Vechten had spoken to me of Toscanini's great period at the Metropolitan: "In those years he would conduct a *Tristan* or *Götterdämmerung* that was overwhelming; but the thing to hear was his performance of early Verdi—of *La Traviata*." And a few days later Toscanini gave millions of radio listeners an idea of what Van Vechten had talked about. These listeners, for whom *La Traviata* had been a discontinuous series of sections pulled out of shape by the vocal exhibitionism to which the conductor had meekly deferred, now heard phrases in which even the tenor's or soprano's climactic high notes were part of the plastically modeled phrase-contours—heard whole acts which by such continuity of pace and sonority from phrase to phrase and section to section were made into coherent entities. In 1935 W. J. Turner, attempting to convey the superiority of a Toscanini performance to those of other conductors, used the analogy of a poem of Keats printed clearly on good paper as against the same poem printed in smudged ink on blotting paper, or a first-class photograph made by an expert with the finest materials as against a poor one made with a mediocre camera by a

---

And Robert Charles Marsh—in his grandly and inaccurately titled *Toscanini and the Art of Orchestral Performance*—added his own confusion and error to Taubman's by omitting Taubman's statement about Toscanini's having *felt* the need of a cadenza, and attributing to Taubman *my* statement about Toscanini's having *recognized* the explicit indications of a cadenza in Mozart's score. "In his book, *The Maestro*," Marsh wrote, "Howard Taubman tells us that Toscanini made this recording for other conductors as a demonstration of how Mozart should be played. Among other things it demonstrated [still, apparently, according to Taubman] that in the slow movement Mozart had clearly indicated a cadenza for the first violin by writing a six-four chord, a rest, and a trill leading back into the melodic line. Haggin reports that when Toscanini heard the Koussevitzky performance, in which the chord, the rest, and the trill were played through exactly as marked, he exclaimed, 'This man is no musician. He is *ignorante!*'"
Such was the writing about Toscanini.

not highly capable person. "The musical impression made by Toscanini when he conducts a work," said Turner, "is incredibly clearer in detail, better proportioned as to parts, and more vivid as a whole, than those made by any other conductor." This was the impression produced by the 1946 *Traviata;* and with its accuracy, clarity and order it had the effect of revelation: one heard the work as one had never heard it before.

I suspected at the time that this performance was slightly different from those Van Vechten heard at the Metropolitan—that in the opera house the performance, although essentially the same in style, had proceeded a little more slowly and with more rhetorical expansiveness, and that in the concert hall, after many years in which Toscanini had been concerned mostly with symphonic music, it was a little swifter and closer-knit. The style of the NBC performance, in other words, was essentially the same, but refined, clarified, and—like that of the November Mozart *Haffner* Symphony—even apotheosized. As for its effect, there were moments which I thought would have gained by the earlier expansiveness, but others which unquestionably gained by the new urgency—notably the first act and the later scene of Flora's party, whose febrile character was excitingly effective and right.

The first act also was tense; and this must have increased the nervousness of Licia Albanese that resulted in her unsteadiness and inaccuracy in *"Sempre libera,"* as against her beautiful singing in the subsequent acts. As for that tension, it should have taught Toscanini something he hadn't known ten years before. When he left the New York Philharmonic, Dusolina Giannini told me he had said he was tired of the routine of four or five rehearsals and three or four concerts week after week—especially the three or four performances of one program; and one attraction of the NBC offer had been that it called for only one performance each week. But the repetitions of the one program with the Philharmonic had had an important value: a conductor and an orchestra may achieve a performance completely at rehearsal; but the first time in public there is likely to be unsettling tension; and relaxed security may come only at the second or third performance. I recall, for example, that when Toscanini conducted the Philharmonic in Beethoven's Ninth in 1936 the performance was tense, driven and harsh-sounding on Thursday and again on Friday, but amazingly relaxed, spacious and beautiful-sounding on Sunday. At NBC there was only the first public performance, in an atmosphere of tension that sometimes made this performance less good than the one at the final rehearsal where conductor and orchestra were at ease; and it was in fact at these rehearsals that one heard some of the greatest of Toscanini's performances. The first act of an opera, then, was likely to suffer from this tension; and the first act of *La Traviata* did.

Thus there were defects in the *Traviata* performance, but not the ones alleged by some critics—not, specifically, the "tempos . . . both fast and rigid" which "thwart [the singers'] efforts." There were fast tempos which were suitable, like the ones in the febrile first act; but there were also tempos—even in the first act—which were suitably slow and plastic; and the beautiful-sounding, plastically and expressively phrased singing of Peerce and Albanese was not that of singers who were being thwarted. Neither, for that matter, was the coarse-sounding singing of Merrill.

As a matter of fact the critics I have just referred to, who specialize in opera, object to all the Verdi performances—the *Otello, Aïda, Falstaff* and *Un Ballo in Maschera* as well as the *Traviata*—that Toscanini broadcast and Victor subsequently issued on records. And I may as well deal with their objections at this point.

The performances they approve of are the usual ones in opera houses, in which the singers are allowed to show off their voices at any cost to shape of phrase and continuity of flow; the performances they disapprove of are the ones in which the singers are held by Toscanini to tempo and shape of phrase. They don't of course express their approval and disapproval in those terms: the self-indulgent singing they call "expressive"; the tempos and style that permit it they call "idiomatic"; and in the Toscanini performance presumably unidiomatic tempos "both fast and rigid" "thwart" the singers' attempts to sing expressively and compel them to sing inexpressively. Virgil Thomson made up in his head a Toscanini who was an opera conductor until the age of fifty, when he had to deal with the symphonic repertory without knowledge of its traditions, and solved the problem by "streamlining" the music; from the opera specialists I have referred to one would get the idea of Toscanini as a symphonic conductor who in his old age, lacking knowledge of what is idiomatic in the performance of Verdi, streamlined *this* music. Nor is it only with excessively fast and rigid tempos that he is alleged to have made it impossible for singers to do more than produce the notes without expressiveness: he is accused also of having preferred inexperienced or undistinguished singers who were willing to submit to his tyranny; and to his accusers' ears the performances betray not only the singers' lack of experience and distinction but their terror of him.

Actually Toscanini's NBC performances of Verdi were those of a man who conducted his first *Aïda* in the opera house in 1886 and his last *Falstaff* there in 1937, and whose stage performances—as I can testify concerning the Salzburg ones of 1937 and the Milan Scala ones of 1929—were like the NBC performances in their freedom from the singers' "idiomatic" distortions that Verdi fought against all his life. Presumably the critics who disapprove of the NBC performances would not have liked the similar *Traviatas* and *Trovatores* that Van Vechten heard at the Metropolitan and treasured in his memory; but they could hardly have attributed those performances to ignorance of either the correct style for Verdi or the traditional distortion of that style in the opera house. Toscanini's Metropolitan performances represented his knowledge of what was truly idiomatic and his repudiation of what was falsely "idiomatic"; and what his critics would not have liked in them represented in addition the personal style of performance (what Virgil Thomson called "streamlining") that he brought to all music—to opera at eighteen, to symphonic music at twenty-eight—a style whose outstanding characteristic in opera as in symphonic music was a coherent plasticity that tended in later years toward greater simplicity, economy, subtlety. His beat, then, was never anything but flexible in relation to the music; in relation to the singer it was unyielding only in compelling her to operate within the beautifully plastic flow it created in the music. And this didn't prevent Destinn or Hempel or Fremstad from singing expressively and beautifully.

Nor did it prevent the singers in his NBC performances from doing so: the mediocre, inexpressive singing of inexperienced, intimidated singers who are driven breathless by excessively fast tempos, which the critics have reported hearing, was—and is, on the Victor records—not there to be heard. Some of the singing is poor; but most of it is good, and some of it is superb. Moreover the majority of the principals are Metropolitan stars; and it is two of these, Albanese and Merrill, who do the poor singing in the *Traviata*, and another, Richard Tucker, whose voice is cold and lusterless in the *Aïda*; whereas it is two of the comparatively unknown singers, Herva Nelli and Giuseppe Valdengo—the chief targets of the critics I have mentioned—who, far from being mediocre and intimidated, contribute some of the performances' most beautiful and expressive singing. Nelli, in the third act of *Aïda*, does sound frightened for a moment in the phrase near the end of "O *patria mia*" that rises to high C; but even a greater singer would be frightened by having to sing the difficult phrase all in one breath, as Nelli had to do. And later in the act Nelli and Tucker *are* driven breathless by the excessively fast tempo of the concluding section of their duet; but this is an exceedingly rare exception to the rightness of pacing, fast and slow, that is one of the things in the performances which produce the effect of revelation.

On February 9 and 16 Toscanini gave the radio public its first hearing of Berlioz's *Romeo and Juliet* in its entirety, together with a scene from *The Damnation of Faust*. And somewhere between the *Traviata* and the *Romeo* I was at Toscanini's home, where I listened with him to the test pressings of what I think was the recording of Mozart's *Jupiter* Symphony. For some reason Toscanini was worried about the recorded sound; and in the end I took the records home with me to hear what they sounded like on my phonograph. Within a day, before I could report back, I had a telephone call from Walter, whom I heard repeating to his father my statement that the sound was good. Then Toscanini himself got on the phone to ask me; and I repeated to him that the sound was good. He seemed still unsatisfied; so I asked him if he would like to hear for himself. Yes, he would; and so a day or two later he arrived at my apartment with Walter, who was loaded down with a stack of records.

I first played the older recording of the *Tristan* finale to establish the sound from my equipment, which Toscanini pronounced a little deficient in bass but otherwise good. He kept moving about restlessly, and Walter suggested: "Relax; sit down"; so he sat down, but didn't relax, and soon was on his feet again. I then played the test pressings that had worried him; and he seemed now to be satisfied with their sound. Then Walter began to put on the additional test pressings he had brought along, of which I remember only the ones of Weber's Overture to *Der Freischütz*. After the first side of this recording, as the second side began to be heard, Toscanini, who at that moment was seated at the piano, cried out: "Is wrong record! Is not same tempo as first record!"; whereupon Walter replaced it with another, and his father, when he heard the first measures, exclaimed: "Now is right tempo!"

Later, still seated at the piano, he pointed to the score of Berlioz's *Romeo* on the music rack and said: "*Love Scene* is most beautiful music in the world."

Romeo was followed by Schubert's C-major; and I remember the rehearsal in which the solo horn, Arthur Berv, played his opening statement with the slight emphasis on the first note of each measure that the score prescribes, but Toscanini compelled him to put the heavier and cruder accents on the notes that can be heard in the recording of the performance, M-1167 and LM-1040. It is interesting that in the 1953 performance on LM-1835 Berv plays his opening statement with only the prescribed slight emphasis once more. And the two recordings enable one to hear also that the 1947 performance still retained features of the 1941 performance with the Philadelphia Orchestra—notably the coda of the first movement—but already had some of the changed features of the 1953 performance—notably the coda of the finale.

Another important event of the 1946–47 series was the performance of Beethoven's Overture *For the Consecration of the House* on March 16, which gave most radio listeners their first hearing of this strange and wonderful piece. And most concertgoers too: my own attendance at concerts in New York began somewhere around 1914; but this was the first public performance of the piece for me. Previously I had known it only from Weingartner's recorded performance; and I could appreciate how fortunate radio listeners were in becoming acquainted with it through Toscanini's performance, with its tempos that were so skillfully chosen, as Weingartner's were not, to be right for each section and to connect the sections in a coherent progression.

Since Toscanini was criticized for persisting in playing those little pieces by Martucci and other minor Italians, let me point out that he also persisted in playing parts and the whole of Berlioz's *Romeo and Juliet* when nobody else did; that he did the same with *Harold in Italy*; that he gave my generation of concert-goers its first experiences of Beethoven's *Missa Solemnis*; and that he now did the same with the *Consecration of the House* Overture. He did play some worthless music, but no more, I am sure, than other conductors did. The difference was that he played worthless music mostly by Italians, whereas the others played worthless music by Germans, Russians and Americans; and I don't agree that this constitutes the difference between bad and good program-making.

He was criticized also for not fulfilling his obligation to living composers; but it should be remembered that he began his almost-thirty-year career as a symphonic conductor in this country at the age of sixty, and that as a young conductor in Italy he did conduct what was new and modern. In opera he conducted the first performances at La Scala of Strauss's *Salome* in 1906 and Debussy's *Pelléas et Mélisande* in 1908; and in the season of 1925–26 he prepared a stage production of Stravinsky's *Petrushka* there which illness prevented him from conducting. And as one of the most active symphonic conductors in Italy he played Strauss's *Till Eulenspiegel* in 1902, *Death and Transfiguration* in 1905, and *Don Juan* in 1906, Debussy's *Faun* piece in 1905, *Nuages* in 1906, *La Mer* in 1912, and *Ibéria* in 1918, Stravinsky's *Petrushka* in 1916, Dukas's *Sorcerer's Apprentice* in 1904, Glazunov's Symphony No. 6 in 1904, Sibelius's *En Saga* in 1905. Even at the Metropolitan he conducted Dukas's *Ariane et Barbe Bleu*. At sixty he may have felt the obligation to living composers was one for younger conductors; and since there were others capable and willing to assume the obligation, it wasn't a bad division of labor to have Stokowski, Koussevitzky, Rodzinski and Mitropoulos handling contemporary works and Toscanini restricting himself to standard repertory. Even so Toscanini did play Shostakovitch's First and Seventh Symphonies, Khabalevsky's Second Symphony and his *Colas Breugnon* Overture. And at the age of seventy-one, astonishingly, he played Barber's *Essay for Orchestra* and *Adagio for Strings*, at seventy-three Roy Harris's Symphony No. 3, at seventy-five Copland's *El Salón México*, and during a couple of years thereafter pieces by Creston, Gould, Gershwin, Gilbert, Kennan, Griffes, William Schuman and Siegmeister.

On the day in April 1947 that I was to visit Toscanini I happened to see someone from Victor who mentioned a few bits of information and gossip. One piece of information was that Toscanini was dissatisfied with the sound of the timpani on a couple of sides of the recording of Tchaikovsky's *Romeo and Juliet*; another was that Victor had induced him to record the Mozart *Haffner* with a reduced orchestra in NBC's Studio 3A, which was smaller than 8H. As for gossip, there had been an NBC Symphony rehearsal of Strauss's *Death and Transfiguration* at which Toscanini had let the orchestra go on playing to the end of the introduction before he exploded in anger at its inaccuracy; and the engineers had recorded this episode and more of the rehearsal, including further explosions. On a later occasion the recording had been played for Toscanini, who had exclaimed: "That's me!" and covered his face with his hands.

As I waited downstairs that afternoon while the maid went up to announce me I could hear the piano being played. The playing stopped; and a few moments later I heard my name called by Toscanini. I looked up and saw him at the top of the stairs, smiling down at me. "Come up," he said; and when I did he led me to his study and sat down again at the piano. In February he had broadcast a scene from Berlioz's *Damnation of Faust*; and it was this opera that he had been playing on the piano now. "I would like to play this next year: is so beautiful! I hear it played by Y——: was terrible!—such tempi!" —and he gave examples at the piano. "But what tenor? Is extremely difficult, tenor part." Turning a few pages of the score, he pointed to a long-sustained high B-flat (I think) and said: "Is very difficult to sing this note. I hear it once in falsetto"; and he proceeded to sing the aria in his croaking singing voice, accompanying himself with piano chords that were sloppily broken between the two hands. "Is so beautiful! And *Romanza* of Marguerite," which he also sang and played. "But what soprano or mezzo-soprano? I think maybe Tourel, because is very important to have somebody who can sing words properly. But is five years since she sing with me in *Romeo and Juliet*, and I do not know how she sing now." I suggested finding out; and I also suggested Ramon Vinay for the tenor part.

Then, "I want to play for you record of Tchaikovsky's *Romeo and Juliet*, because in this place"—and he played a passage on the piano—"timpani are too weak, and I want to put in more timpani"—by which he meant that he wanted Victor to dub a new side from the old one and at the same time dub in additional live timpani sound. He then played the test pressing of the Tchaikovsky *Romeo* for me, putting on each record himself clumsily while I watched apprehensively, and once putting on a wrong record with the Khabalevsky *Colas Breugnon* Overture. Seated this time, he conducted the performance as always, giving entrances, anticipating points, smiling his pleasure at what he heard, exclaiming once: "Is good, crescendo of *violini*, no?" And he pointed out the unsatisfactory timpani sound: "Only *celli* and *bassi* are clear." "But I hear the timpani," I said. "Yes, but is weak." I pointed out that if the two sides were dubbed to put in additional timpani sound there would be a loss of some of the beauty of all the other sound, as there had been from the similar dubbing of one side of Haydn's No. 98—which he didn't remember. As I spoke he nodded his understanding, but not, it turned out, his agreement; for when I finished he said: "But I cannot let people say I do not know right sound of timpani."

There being nothing more to say about this, he remembered the recording of the Mozart *Haffner*, which he hadn't listened to yet. "First movement and finale of old *Haffner* are good," he said, "but not Andante and Minuetto: tempi are too slow." Then he played the new first movement, but stopped the Andante after a few moments: "Is wrong take. There is another take with right tempo." Finding the other, he was pleased by it, and by the rest of the recording. "When Bruno Walter conduct *Haffner* at La Scala I do not understand slow tempo of Minuetto. I ask Casals: 'Is correct, Minuetto so slow?'" And I gathered that Casals had fortified him in his conviction that his own faster tempo was right.

"Can you hear is small orchestra?" he asked. "No," I answered, "but I can hear it is a small studio." At which he told me how difficult it had been to play in that studio, which he didn't like and wouldn't record in again. (Actually he did record the Haydn *Clock* Symphony there too. According to my Victor informant, RCA [of which Victor and NBC were subsidiary companies] had insisted on Victor using NBC's Studio 3A for certain reasons; and the result was two of the most atrocious Toscanini recordings ever issued—with harsh sound and an acoustic deadness that struck the ear a blow after a loud chord. And later the LP dubbings were made unlistenable by Victor's "enhancement.")

Next he played the test pressing of the Schumann *Manfred* Overture. "You like *Manfred* Overture?" he asked. "Very much," I answered. "Is beautiful music!" he exclaimed. "But Downes say is not good music! Ah, *Dio santo!*" And he played on the piano a passage from a Beethoven sonata that Downes had said Schumann borrowed. I no longer recall the passage, but remember saying, as Toscanini nodded agreement, that Schumann might be echoing something but certainly made it his own.

With this, Toscanini stopped playing records, which he said tired him. Looking about him in search of something, he exclaimed "Ah!" and picked up from his desk the pocket score of Mozart's Divertimento. I had asked him in a letter whether he would transfer his markings into another copy of the score for me (my score of Berlioz's *Romeo* has Toscanini's markings for the placing and removal of the strings' mutes in the *Love Scene*); and he now said: "Here is score of Divertimento. I do not have cadenza; I will find it at NBC. Is here cadenza"—as he pointed to the faint traces of some musical notation that had been written in the score and then erased—"but I make different one which must be at NBC. I will find it and send it to you." I explained that I had wanted him to transfer his markings from this copy to another. "No, you take this one."

Then we sat down to talk; and he asked: "You work hard this year?"—referring to the fact that I had begun that year a weekly column on radio music for the Sunday *Herald Tribune*. "Yes," I answered. "There have been two articles to write each week instead of one; and I write very slowly." He nodded as I spoke, and said: "Is better so. Is better to make slow and *good*, as to make fast and not good."

Walter Toscanini arrived; and his father told him that we had listened to the Tchaikovsky *Romeo*, and that the timpani must be reinforced. Again I pointed out the loss in the other sound from dubbing; and he answered: "You have better ear; I will not hear it." I repudiated this amazing statement; whereupon it turned out that he had meant my ear for recorded sound; but I insisted that he would hear the loss, and suggested that he play the finale of the Haydn No. 98, in which he would hear the loss in the first side as against the second. But it was still impossible for him to let the *Romeo* go out with the timpani not right. So we agreed that the thing to do was to make the dubbings and let him decide then whether he preferred the dubbed sides or the originals.

There were questions and comments about performances he had heard. "Did you hear broadcast of Santa Monica Orchestra with Rachmilovich? I do not know anything about this conductor; but I listen—I hear—strings—whole orchestra—is good. I am glad to hear young conductor who play good." And to Walter: "You must tell Chotzie[11] to bring him to NBC for

[11] Samuel Chotzinoff.

summer concerts." On the other hand another conductor, who had been highly recommended to him, "make terrible tempi." And Z——, who formerly "was cold, but conduct correct [illustrated by precise conducting gestures], now stop beating time [illustrated], then make big movement [again illustrated]. And tempi in *Ibéria!* [Toscanini put his hand to his head in pain.] He play second movement so slow that this *passage* [the chromatically descending and ascending passage soon after the beginning] is so [illustrated at the piano]. *Dio santo!*" Then something reminded him of Sibelius's Seventh Symphony: "I listen with score. Sometime you must show me where is music. *I* cannot hear any music in this piece."

Had he, I asked, heard the De Sabata recording of Mozart's *Requiem,* which I thought was so remarkable. He nodded as I spoke, and answered: "Is good performance. De Sabata is good but sometimes nervous conductor." (But on another occasion he used a term of disapproval instead of "nervous" for De Sabata's violent gesticulation. Mentioning that he had been accused of not doing enough for young conductors, he said: "I always invite young conductors to come to my rehearsals. De Sabata come to my rehearsals—but then on podium is Pagliaccio!")

"Did you hear A——?" he asked. "Only a little of the *Coriolan* Overture and *Daphnis and Chloë,* which I didn't like," I said. "Did you hear Berlioz *Fantastique?*"—referring to the performance with which A—— had created a sensation. "No. I hear only part of last movement on record," said Toscanini. "Is in double tempo. Is easy to make exciting in double tempo. But is so fast, *tromboni* cannot play correct this *passage* [he played it on the piano]; also violas here [he played the passage on the piano]." Walter had found the record, an acetate made in Carnegie Hall during the performance; and when he played it Toscanini pointed to the inaccurate playing of the trombones and violas. "Is easy to make exciting in double tempo," he repeated at the end, "but not easy to play correct." And I believe it was on this occasion that he said of the work itself: "I never like *Fantastique:* is for me not good music. Only last two movements are good music. Once, in Lago Maggiore, at night, I hear on radio

Fantastique—I do not know who conduct—is so beautiful I think maybe is good music. I look in score: is not good music. I never know who is conductor of this performance!"

Toscanini's mind reverted to Berlioz's *Damnation of Faust*; and we all discussed my suggestion of Vinay. Toscanini now remembered the matter of time. He added up the time required by the scenes that would make up the first broadcast and found that they would fit into the available hour; but the second part turned out to be too long; and Toscanini speculated whether the program following the NBC Symphony would give up a quarter of an hour this one time. He began to figure out the time again, while Walter remarked to me: "What my father does not understand is that there must be a decision *now*, because singers must be engaged before they get involved with other activities." Tourel was mentioned again, and Toscanini repeated: "I must have somebody who can sing words. Is not enough, beautiful voice: must be expression. No singer understand that."

The subject of singers with nothing but voices, and their musical excesses in the display of those voices, reminded him of a De Lucia record which he asked Walter to play. While he was getting it his father played on the piano some of the phrases as De Lucia distorted them; and when the record was played Toscanini sat laughing at them. But Caruso's name caused him to hold his head in his hands: "He sing with me at La Scala in '99, and I write to Boito: 'You must come to La Scala to hear *Elisir d'Amore* with young tenor who sing like angel.' But in 1901 is already change; and in New York——! I tell him: 'Yes, you make much money—but no! *no! NO!!*'"

It was now late in the afternoon, and Toscanini left us for a few minutes. When he returned he had changed from his maroon smoking jacket to his usual black suit. He was driving down to dinner with Mr. and Mrs. Vladimir Horowitz, his son-in-law and daughter, and offered me a lift. While we waited for the car he showed Walter a book—with a long inscription by him—that he was taking to little Sonia Horowitz. "Is very good," he said to Walter, his face expressing his delight over it.

In the car I asked him about Schuch, a former director of

the Dresden Opera, whom someone had mentioned to me; and his face lighted up: "Oh yes! Is *good!* Is *good* opera conductor! He came to La Scala—is good conductor of Italian opera. I also hear him in Dresden—I hear *Oberon*—I remember overture is very beautiful, and I am *sure* is change in strings. When Busch come to La Scala I say: 'Look in score of *Oberon* and tell me if is change in strings.'"

What about Nikisch? "Is good conductor—but make performance for public [he made gestures of acting]. And sometimes he do not look at score." Then with increasing intensity: "When I conduct I am always prepared. I do not stand before public to show I am Toscanini—never! Always I try to do my best. And always conducting is great suffering for me. At home, with score, when I play piano, is great happiness. But with orchestra is great suffering—*sempre, sempre!*[12] Even when I listen to record I am afraid horn will not play correct, clarinet will make mistake—*sempre, sempre!* Last week they play for me record of rehearsal of *Tod und Verklärung*. I do not know why they make this record. All my life I have bad temper: is impossible for me to understand why orchestra cannot play correct. But when I hear this record I am ashamed."

Later he asked again about my work; and as I described how I had made things harder for myself by undertaking to give a lecture which I had given before, but which I had now found had to be changed, Toscanini nodded and smiled his understanding. He asked how long I had been writing for the *Herald Tribune;* and I said since the preceding October. "I read some interesting things in these articles," he said. "Do you also read the *Nation* articles?" I asked. "Oh yes! . . . People write to you?" "Yes," I said, "from all over the country; and it's a great pleasure—especially the letters from young people, sometimes very extraordinary young people, and from small places." His face had been expressing his own pleasure at this; and he said: "You write about this man . . . [he groped for the name] is professor . . . in university . . . here"—and he pointed northward from Ninety-fifth Street where we were at the moment. "Columbia?" I suggested. "Columbia, *sì.*"

[12] always

"Lang?" "Lang, sì." He was referring to a *Nation* article in which I had, among other things, quoted from a letter in which a reader cited the factual record of the number of performances and number of seasons, against Lang's statement in his *Music in Western Civilization* that Auber's opera *La Muette de Portici* was forgotten shortly after its initial success. "In that article," I said to Toscanini, "the letter I quoted was from one of those young people—from Greensboro, North Carolina." He nodded; then, pursuing his own thought, he said: "The musicologists—they know everything——" "Except music," we concluded in unison.

I visited Toscanini again in mid-October 1947; and on the way upstairs to his study I heard him playing over and over again the little ascending scale of the woodwinds at the beginning of Beethoven's *Consecration of the House* Overture. It turned out that he was going to broadcast the piece again on the twenty-fifth, and was preparing as usual by going over the score and listening to the recording of the performance of the preceding March. He showed me in the score the places that were creating problems and difficulties—the bassoon part in one tutti, for example, about which he said, shaking his head dejectedly: "I try everything, but I am afraid I will never hear these bassoons." And then with the score open before us we listened to the recording of the earlier performance.

I remember only one other matter that came up that morning. In July NBC had announced that in October the NBC Symphony broadcasts would be moved from Sunday at five to Saturday at six-thirty; and I had written in the *Herald Tribune* that if NBC was right in contending that a greater number of stations would carry the program at the new time, this was only because the time had little commercial value—which was to say that it was a time when people were at dinner or preparing for dinner or on the way out to dinner, and in any case not able to listen to the radio. In September I had discussed the matter again in the *Herald Tribune*, quoting readers in the Midwest and West who had written me that the broadcasts, if carried live, would reach those areas at earlier times when some people were at work. Moreover, in mid-October Toscanini had not yet begun his broadcasts, and the orchestra was still playing under its summer conductors. I was therefore amazed, when Toscanini mentioned the matter that morning, to discover he was under the impression that several million more people were listening on Saturday than had listened on Sunday.

I think this was one of the times I was asked to stay for lunch; and I remember the servant attempting, without success, to coax Toscanini to take some veal in addition to the few vegetables that were all he ate.

With the *Consecration of the House* Overture Toscanini, on the twenty-fifth, played Beethoven's Seventh; and I recall the performance of the finale at a rehearsal. His movements at rehearsal were more uninhibitedly vigorous than they were in the presence of an audience at a concert; and the climax of the last crescendo had him stamping his feet—with results that caused one member of the orchestra to exclaim: "I've got to get back into my skin." On the other hand the first measures of Mendelssohn's rarely heard *Tale of Lovely Melusine* Overture were played, at a rehearsal the following week, with an inflection so exquisite as to bring tears to my eyes. And Mendelssohn's pieces for *A Midsummer Night's Dream* were played with an exquisite plasticity and grace, and on occasion an elegantly impassioned animation, which I found equally moving.

A Mozart program included the Divertimento K.287 again and the Bassoon Concerto K.191, both of which were recorded. I imagine the concerto was written for some bassoon-player Mozart knew; and I would suspect that Mozart used the occasion to amuse himself—not only obviously with the tootling and braying he gave to the solo instrument, but subtly with the comments he gave to the orchestra—comments which go unnoticed in the usual performance, but which claimed delighted attention with the life they had from Toscanini's inflection.

And a subsequent Handel-Vivaldi-Bach program had one wondering why, if Toscanini played a Handel concerto grosso with a small chamber group, he played a Bach suite with all the NBC strings; why, with this mass of strings, he didn't use a piano that would have been heard instead of a harpsichord that was inaudible; why he played an uninteresting little violin concerto of Vivaldi instead of one of the many lovely works of this composer that he might have played; and why he played the monstrous Respighi transcription of Bach's *Passacaglia* for organ.

The climax of the fall series came on December 1 and 8 with the performance of Verdi's *Otello*. The art which manifests itself in astounding fashion in as early a work as *Macbeth*, in the vocal and orchestral writing of the *Sleepwalking Scene* —this art achieves in *Otello* a sustained incandescent invention that fills in moment after moment with marvelously wrought details of melody, harmony, figuration and orchestration. And this sustained operation of Verdi's powers was given overwhelming effect by the similar sustained operation of the powers that kept the progression unfailingly beautiful in sound, clear in outline and texture, and continuous in impetus, tension and force. In this performance Toscanini had an all but perfect cast; and so one heard—and still hears on Victor LM-6107—not only the orchestral part superbly played but the vocal parts with the tonal beauty and remarkable expressive inflection and coloring of Valdengo's singing, the loveliness and purity of Nelli's, the fine singing of Vinay at the times—notably in the third act—when he achieved delicacy without disturbing effort, and ringing sonority without a disturbing quaver.

At the rehearsals of the orchestra alone Toscanini filled in the singing—with no vocal beauty but with much expressive force. I still remember his delivery of Iago's "*Non so*"[13] in reply to Otello's question what had happened, after the drunken brawl in the first act. And I remember also his stopping the orchestra in the third-act duet of Otello and Desdemona to say: "You must understand this situation: these are her first tears."

Before I visited Toscanini early in February 1948 I asked

[13] "I don't know."

to hear some of the recording of the broadcast of Berlioz's *Romeo and Juliet* a year earlier. But when I arrived Toscanini had an acetate recording of A——'s entire performance of the Berlioz *Fantastique* with which to demonstrate to me that other parts were as bad as the finale. "I pay for recording, to have proof!" he exclaimed—proof that the march movement, which he proceeded to play for me, also was whipped up in tempo in a way that was exciting but that converted the *March to the Scaffold* into a march of triumph—something he regarded as not just a musical but a moral transgression.

With this demonstrated, Toscanini sat down with me at the piano with the score of *Romeo* open before us, to listen to the recording of the broadcast. I listened and read; he conducted, gave entrance cues, sang, and occasionally pointed to something in the score, exclaiming: "This is *honest* performance: you can read it in score!"

Later, as he was putting away the score, he looked at me with a smile and said: "Now, Haggin, what would you like?"

"Anything you would like to hear," I answered.

"No"—still smiling—"what would you like—what would you like to have?" And as I stared at him uncomprehendingly he added: "You come only to see me?"

"Yes, of course," I managed to answer, so shocked that I didn't until later apprehend what he was telling me in this way; but then I did see what a revealing incident this was. My meetings with Toscanini were few and infrequent and limited in scope; and I didn't get to know him as his intimates did; but I did get to know him as I did—meaning that I think I learned some things about him which I feel sure of, no matter how they may appear to someone else. Those who have read the description of Toscanini's behavior in the Chotzinoff book may find it hard to accept the idea of his essential innocence; but I am thinking of a child's innocence which is sometimes retained up to the point where the young person comes face to face with some of the brutal and evil realities of adult existence and resorts to defenses and counterattacks that may be unpleasant. I got an impression of such innocence in Toscanini; and I find it understandable that coming face to face with a world of hard-eyed people who all wanted something from him—for whom he was in one way or another an object of exploitation—he occasionally dealt with them in the ways described by Chotzinoff. Even with friends? Even with friends: apparently he sensed what sort of friends some of them were. And to me it is significant that Chotzinoff in his book describes Toscanini as unfailingly courteous and considerate to servants.

After the playing of the Berlioz *Romeo* recording and the incident I have just described there was the usual chatting about what we had heard. Ansermet had been conducting the NBC Symphony for the first time; and Toscanini pronounced him "best conductor of NBC"—which I took to mean the best of the guest conductors the orchestra had had. "Is good musician. When he play *La Valse* is different from my *La Valse*, and Chotzinoff say is not good. But I say: 'No. Is not like my *La Valse*—but is good.'" As for the music Ansermet had played, Stravinsky's *Symphonies pour instruments à vent* had impressed him as the work of a mathematician (it may have been on this occasion that he said he had stopped playing Stravinsky because "he call Beethoven fake"—clearly a misconstruction of whatever Stravinsky had said). Nor had he cared for Debussy's *Jeux*. Ansermet had also played Debussy's *Gigues*; and this visit may have been one of the several times when I asked Toscanini whether he had ever played *Gigues* and *Rondes de printemps*, the companion pieces of *Ibéria*, and each time, nodding and smiling reminiscently, he answered: "Ye-e-es, Debussy send me score," and nothing more. Late in March *Rondes de printemps* was announced for a Debussy program, but didn't materialize.

Since he was to play Tchaikovsky's *Manfred* in a few weeks this work was in his mind, and he told me why he liked it best of Tchaikovsky's music. "Is not one note banal. Not like Fifth—Fifth is banal: second movement—ah-h-h, *Dio santo!*" He mentioned that he was going to play Beethoven's Ninth at his last broadcast. And the opera next year would be Verdi's *Falstaff*.

At some point I asked him his opinion of Frieda Hempel, whose recordings had given me an impression of her as the greatest singer of her time. "Was good Eva in *Meistersinger*," he said; and he remembered also her Page in *Un Ballo in Maschera*, her singing in Beethoven's Ninth. The soloists in this performance of the Ninth at the Metropolitan—Hempel, Homer, Karl Jörn, Putnam Griswold—were "best I ever have; and was good orchestra." This reminded him of the rehearsal at which the Metropolitan orchestra "play like pig" and he swore at it in Italian. When, subsequently, the Italian was translated, the orchestra was offended and said it wouldn't play for him until he apologized. To the mediator who came to see him Toscanini explained that he couldn't apologize because "orchestra play like pig." But he proposed the solution that worked: "I go to rehearsal and smile and say 'Good morning.'"

I had been asked to stay for lunch; and when Toscanini and I seated ourselves at the table Walter Toscanini wasn't there. "Is good," Toscanini commented, "but not punctual. Only once was punctual: I was married June 21; he was born March 21."

Of the further talk at lunch I remember only a few fragments. At one point Toscanini spoke of Puccini as not having been "sincere" in relation to the words as Verdi had been—except in the finale of *La Bohème*. At another point the name of Cleofonte Campanini came up; and Toscanini spoke highly of his ability as a conductor: "Had taste in Italian opera, but could not read score. First rehearsal is good; but he make more rehearsal and make worse," and he chuckled. Koussevitzky's name also came up: Toscanini thought he should have stopped conducting, and suspected that "he conduct because I conduct. I will conduct until I am ninety!"—this with an emphatic jab of his arm toward the floor. And Koussevitzky's actions as a world figure elicited from Toscanini the comment "I am not great man! Is enough to be a man!"

He was driving down to NBC for a rehearsal of the soloists for the Ninth Symphony; and I drove with him part of the way. I remember only mentioning something done by his extraordinary first cellist, Frank Miller, and Toscanini's face lighting up as he agreed that Miller was a fine musician—and, he added, his first viola, Carlton Cooley, too.

On March 6 Toscanini broadcast the only performance of Mozart's Symphony K.543 in E flat that he ever gave with an American orchestra. It was a performance, on the one hand, filled with the exquisite inflection he so well understood how to put in between the *p*'s and *f*'s; but a performance, on the other hand, sacrificed to a cause—the cause of the true Andante. The common error of taking Andante to mean slow, and of playing a Mozart Andante, in effect, as an Adagio, had become an obsession with Toscanini; and instead of playing the Andante movement of the E-flat Symphony as a true Andante in terms of its substance, he made the performance a demonstration of a true Andante in terms of the 2/4 time signature—with results that can be heard on Victor LM-2001, which reproduces the performance that was broadcast: the Andante in terms of the two beats in each measure was much too fast for the proper flow and articulation of the substance. The obsession about even slow tempos being too slow caused him also to play the Adagio introduction of the first movement a little too fast for the music to have the majesty it should have. And the obsession about everything being too slow produced an Allegretto tempo in the Minuet that was too fast for the music to have its proper grace.

On March 20 the owners of television sets wherever the NBC telecast was carried by local stations were able not only to hear but to see Toscanini and the NBC Symphony perform a Wagner program. Like the OWI film of performances of Verdi's Overture to *La Forza del Destino* and *Hymn of the Nations*, the telecast followed the usual film practice of shifting back and forth between conductor and players. The moments in which one saw Toscanini at close range as his first-desk string-players saw him, and not only observed but felt the intensity of his involvement, were moving and exciting; and some of the goings-on in the orchestra were interesting. But because Toscanini was not kept uninterruptedly in view, the listening spectator did not witness what was so fascinating in the Toscanini operation—the related continuities of his activity and the performance it produced.

The continuity in the performance I have referred to many

times: it was, first, one of impetus and tension, which caused the progression of sound, once started, to keep going with unfailing momentum and cohesive tension from one sound to the next; it was, in addition, one of shape, produced by changes of sonority and pace that were always in right proportion to what preceded and followed, so that the timing and force of one sound strongly implied the timing and force of the next, giving the flow naturalness and inevitability in addition to its coherence. This continuous flow of the performance was produced by a continuous activity—a continuous exercise by Toscanini of the utmost attentiveness, concentration and control. Once he started the progression going, he marshaled it along, watched over it, controlled it to make it come out as planned. The marshaling was done with those large, plastic, sensitive movements of his right arm (extended to the point of his baton), which delineated for the orchestra the flow of sound in much of its subtly inflected detail and literally conducted the orchestra from one sound to the next in that flow—the effectiveness of these movements being due to their extraordinary explicitness in conveying his wish at every moment, and to the compelling personal force they transmitted. The left hand meanwhile was in constant activity as the instrument of the apprehensive watchfulness that showed itself on Toscanini's face—now exhorting, now quieting, now warning, now suppressing.

The moment-to-moment relation of the continuities of activity and performance was, I have said, fascinating to watch. And moving in addition was the absorbed, unself-conscious operation of extraordinary powers that gave Toscanini's conducting the appearance of a natural act like a bird's flight, in which the powers operated with complete adequacy for each momentary situation but with no more than adequacy—an economy that was a form of honesty in relation to the material and situation and gave the operation a moral quality.

In this first telecast some of the shifts from Toscanini to the orchestra were well chosen and timed; but sometimes the camera reached the player late, or even too late; it also did some aimless wandering about, and some picking out of players who weren't doing anything that called for this attention; and it failed sometimes to pick out a player who was doing something of great importance.

The April 3 telecast of Beethoven's Ninth was in all respects better. There were longer images of Toscanini's conducting; some of the shifts from him to the orchestra or chorus or soloist were made by a slow dissolve which carried his movements into the playing or singing they were related to, so that the playing or singing became a continuation of his activity; and in some instances the image of Toscanini conducting was kept superimposed on the image of the players or singers. There was less aimless wandering of the camera, and better marksmanship wherever it was aimed. Nevertheless the horn solo in the Trio of the Scherzo was missed both times, and this after the kettledrum joke in the *Ritmo di tre battute* section of the Scherzo had also been missed both times; and I was fuming about all this during the return of the Scherzo, when suddenly there was Toscanini signaling the drummer for the first *forte* statement of the three-note figure, then the drummer playing the figure *forte*, and again *forte*, and again *forte*, and then—after an unexpected extra measure—an unexpected *mezzo-forte*.

What remains in my memory is one image: of Toscanini, at the end of the first movement, lowering his arm and at the same time lowering his eyes in momentary relaxation of bodily and mental tension, then raising his eyes which flashed an electrifying signal to the orchestra as he raised his arm for the second movement.

The performance of the Ninth on this occasion was in Toscanini's later, less expansive style, of which it provided one of the finest, most effective examples. Unfortunately he had undistinguished soloists in the finale.

But he was even more unfortunate in the benefit performance of Verdi's *Requiem* in Carnegie Hall on April 26. In the unaccompanied passage for soprano and chorus just before the concluding fugue, Herva Nelli became separated from the chorus in pitch by an ever widening gap. One expected Toscanini to stop and begin the section again; but he went on, providing a striking example of his iron self-discipline in public in the face of mistakes by his musicians or annoyances from the audience, as compared with his lack of self-control at rehearsals. The commotion at the opening *Fidelio* of the Salzburg Festival in 1937—caused by the presence of the Windsors —was such that I expected him to throw down his baton and walk out; but he went on conducting the performance.

Six of the broadcasts in the fall of 1948 were devoted to a Brahms cycle noteworthy for the fact that the performances of the Haydn Variations and the Third and Fourth Symphonies exhibited once more the repose, the relaxation, the steadiness, and as a result the spaciousness and grandeur they had not had two or three years before. Especially impressive in this way was the concluding passacaglia movement of the Fourth, whose effect—the cumulative force and impact of the series of varied repetitions of the initial eight-measure statement—depends on maintaining the tempo of this initial statement throughout the series of variations, as Brahms directs. This effect is destroyed by the usual practice of changing the tempo in each variation and slowing down enormously in Variations 10 to 15; but Toscanini achieved it in impressive fashion by maintaining the single tempo, with only subtle modifications, throughout the movement.

The relaxation, spaciousness and clarification continued to be evident in the performances of other music in the remaining two broadcasts of the fall series, including one of Strauss's *Don Quixote*. "That," remarked an NBC musician after the final rehearsal of the Strauss piece, "is something we'll never hear the like of again." He was referring to the marvelous clarity of the detail in the complex texture, the plastic beauty of the form in sound; and actually these were heard again in the performance Toscanini broadcast in November 1953, which was issued by Victor on LM-2026. But my musician was right: I have never heard a performance by another conductor that had this clarity and plastic beauty. However I did hear a performance—by Bruno Walter with the New York Symphony in the twenties—which made me laugh more with its sharper pointing up of the fun in the piece. And listening to a recording of Toscanini's performance in 1938 I was amazed by the greater energy it exhibited right from the opening high-spirited statement of the oboe and flute. This lessened energy showed itself in some other performances of the later years, but not in all.

Toscanini was followed by Ansermet, and Ansermet by Guido Cantelli. Listening to Toscanini in those years, and marveling at his continuing powers, one had realized that some day there would nevertheless be an end, and had wondered if there would ever again be the accidental coming together of the particular musical taste, technical capacities and personal characteristics that had combined to produce this unique way of operating as a conductor and its unique results. And so it was exciting to hear in Cantelli's performances with the NBC Symphony an operation similar to Toscanini's in attitude, method and result. The performances, like Toscanini's, shaped the works strictly on the lines laid out by the composers' directions about tempo and dynamics in the score; the shaped progressions resembled Toscanini's in their purity of taste and style, their continuity and organic coherence, their clarity of outline, texture and structure. There were of course differences too: as against the power creating a continuous tension in the flow of a Toscanini performance, one heard in Cantelli's performances a youthful lyricism and grace. These qualities of youth the performances exhibited, but not the immaturity about which some critics felt safe in pontificating to show their keen discernment ("That degree of musical culture and experience which can settle, almost instinctively, on proper tempi and sonorous values for such works as the Mozart are not yet his," observed Irving Kolodin out of the implied fullness of his own musical culture and experience, concerning a beautifully paced and phrased performance of Mozart's Divertimento K.287): the performances certainly would change in time, but each as it was produced then emerged as a completely, satisfyingly achieved entity.

The performances also resembled Toscanini's in their precision of orchestral execution and sonority, their brilliant virtuosity; and if anyone points out that Cantelli was, after all, conducting a virtuoso orchestra, the answer is that such an orchestra plays in that way only for a virtuoso conductor.

One heard in the performances the authority of directing mind and hand that was evident at rehearsals: the authority of the kind of knowledge of everything in the score and everything going on in the orchestra, of one's purpose and the means of achieving this purpose, that commands the respect and response of an orchestra like the NBC Symphony. And Cantelli's musical and technical equipment, his fanatical personal dedication, won this respect and response not only from the conscientious musicians in the orchestra but from the hard-boiled specimens of the genus New York orchestral player.

I believe that in a letter to Toscanini at this time I included the question whether I might attend Cantelli's rehearsals; and when he telephoned he said: "Yes, come to rehearsal. You must hear this young conductor." I had missed the first rehearsal, but got to the second, at which Cantelli worked with the orchestra on Hindemith's *Mathis der Maler*. He did so under several handicaps, one of which was the awareness of Toscanini himself listening in the sixth row behind him. But if this contributed to Cantelli's nervousness and tenseness, it also was a help: the demands of a high-strung, fanatically dedicated person, the fact that he was a young man facing the orchestra of the world's most celebrated conductor, his handicap of not knowing a word of English—all these created not only tenseness in Cantelli but tense situations with the orchestra, which Toscanini's presence prevented from developing into anything worse.

Toscanini's presence also provided the orchestra with amusement. At the first rehearsal he had been given the score of *Mathis*, which he soon knew by memory; and thereafter, completely unconscious of what he was doing, he sat conducting the piece—beating time, signaling entrances, and all the rest. And the same thing happened a week later at the rehearsals of Bartók's *Concerto for Orchestra*.

The program of Toscanini's first broadcast after Cantelli's engagement constituted an additional compliment to the young conductor: a recognition that this time Toscanini was returning to an orchestra which had been kept at the high pitch of technical performance that enabled him to play Berlioz—and not just the *Roman Carnival* Overture and *Harold in Italy*, which require the utmost precision in execution and balanced sonority, but the terrifyingly difficult *Queen Mab* Scherzo, with its feathery string *pianissimos*, glints of woodwind color, and magical sounds of distant horns. And it occurred to me this time that in addition to the imagination, the ear and the technical powers there was one other characteristic of Toscanini that made him so effective a conductor of Berlioz—one related to an outstanding characteristic of Berlioz himself. Nothing that happens in Berlioz's music is perfunctory: when an instrument enters or an inner voice moves, the activity is something attentively, purposefully, freshly thought—this fresh thinking from point to point being responsible for much of the music's ever-amazing originality. In whatever happens one is aware of Berlioz's mind working; and this activity in the music makes it excitingly alive—as it was especially when conducted by Toscanini, in whose performances too one heard nothing done perfunctorily, everything done with attention and energy by a mind unceasingly active.

The spring series was made notable by a Beethoven *Eroica* —in the simpler, swifter, tauter style—that was hair-raising in its energy and power; and on the other hand by a Schubert *Unfinished* remarkable in the way its steady tempos created an almost superearthly quiet and calm in which both the dramatic force and the serenity of the work were achieved. And the series ended with a performance of *Aïda*, on March 26 and April 2, whose accuracy, clarity and order caused this much-battered work also to sound as though it were newly created. Not only did it give artistic validity and effect to the surviving formulas of the earlier Verdi style, but it allowed one to hear beautifully realized the exquisite harmonic and orchestral details with which *Aïda* is enriched, and which Verdi's subtilized craftsmanship elaborated into the fluent idiom of *Otello*.

Except for Tucker, whose voice was powerful but cold and lusterless, the cast was excellent, with Nelli and Valdengo again, and a newcomer, Eva Gustavson, who revealed in the second broadcast the luscious contralto voice that nervousness clouded with tremolo in the first. Nervousness also made Nelli's voice weak and breathy in the first broadcast (portions of the rehearsals, in which Nelli and Gustavson were at ease, appear to have been substituted in Victor LM-6132, with passages that were re-recorded in 1954). And an additional reason for the nervousness on this occasion was the fact that the performance was televised. It was, in fact, filmed, and could be shown again.

The *Aïda* performance was still in Toscanini's mind when I visited him in April. In fact, the first thing he did was to give me a photostat of the passage in the letter in which Verdi added the low B-flats at the end of "*Celeste Aïda*" that are heard in the performance in LM-6132. "I do not know why Verdi did not change the published score," said Toscanini. "Is impossible to sing high B-flat *pianissimo*—only in falsetto, which is not correct style in this work."

I spoke enthusiastically about certain exquisite details in *Aïda*; and Toscanini, who was seated at the piano, played not only the ones I mentioned but others—among them the violins at the beginning of the Nile Scene and the alternations of major and minor in the dance in the Temple Scene. Verdi, he said, was a great artist in addition to being the great melodist that Bellini and Donizetti were—and that only the Italians were, not the Germans. This he demonstrated by first pounding out on the piano the endless sequences at the beginning of the *Liebestod* in *Tristan und Isolde*, breaking off with a vehement "*Dio santo!*", and then playing "*Spirito gentil*" from Donizetti's *La Favorita*, with his face registering his pleasure.

I said I thought Aïda was the most taxing soprano part in the operatic repertory; and he agreed that it was very difficult, especially if the soprano sang the long phrases in "*O patria mia*"—and here he played the one near the end that rises to high C and the concluding phrase that rises to A—in one breath as they are marked, and as Nelli had done.

What about the next opera—what about *Falstaff?* "I would like very much to perform this opera, and I would also like to perform it in little theater in Bussetto in 1952 and to record this performance. But it depend on singers." He mentioned one baritone he had found unsuitable; another who "could sing—but is lazy." And once more he said: "In this opera pronunciation of words is most important."

And *The Damnation of Faust?* "Is no tenor. The high B-flat —though it could be in falsetto, because is the style."

Cantelli also was very much in Toscanini's mind. "I love this young conductor," he said, his face glowing at the thought of Cantelli. "I think is like me when I was young." Nevertheless he had rejected the NBC suggestion to drop Ansermet the following year and give an additional four weeks to Cantelli. "Ansermet is good conductor; and I do not want people to say I bring only Italian conductor."

He thanked me for the copy of W. J. Turner's *Beethoven* I had sent him, and agreed that there were wonderful things in it. I told him about Turner's other writings, including his remarkable pieces about Toscanini's concerts in London. Toscanini said he hadn't met Turner there: "I meet man who write about Wagner"—meaning Ernest Newman. I then told him how, when I had met Turner in London in 1937, he hadn't pretended an interest he didn't feel; how surprised, therefore, I had been in 1943 by a letter from him congratulating me on my writing in *The Nation*; and how pleased and moved I had been to receive this appreciation that was so completely unexpected. "Yes! And so spontaneous!" Toscanini exclaimed, his face lighting up.

I asked him about a statement concerning the appoggiatura that I had found marked by him in Lilli Lehmann's autobiography, which he had lent me. I remember his answering— illustrating at the piano with the opening section of the Overture to *Don Pasquale*—that there had to be variety in the treatment of the appoggiatura, "and this is matter of taste, which conductor must have." And he cited the appoggiaturas in the aria in the second act of Gluck's *Orfeo*, which "Bruno Walter make always the same." The German manner of treating the appoggiatura that he considered wrong was, he said, started by Mahler. "Was crazy man! Fourth Symphony [which presumably he had heard on the radio a day or two before] is terrible!"

I also asked him about a Sunday article of Olin Downes in the early thirties—a report of a conversation with Toscanini, in which Downes quoted him as saying that Berlioz's orchestration was original but not good—that of a genius but an amateur, compared with Wagner—and that it was nonsense to say Rimsky-Korsakov's editing had spoiled Musorgsky's *Boris*—that on the contrary, without Rimsky we wouldn't have had *Boris*. He didn't recall this conversation and remembered only meeting Downes when he conducted the Scala Orchestra in Boston. "Then he was all right; but later—*Dio santo!* I do not understand this man, who write this much [indicating with his fingers a volume a half-inch thick] about my performance of *Otello*, and then praise Metropolitan *Otello*. . . ." Then, coming back to Musorgsky's *Boris*, he conceded that Rimsky's correction of the consecutive fifths in the Simpleton's song had spoiled the passage, but insisted that the editing as a whole had made the work a success. I cited Rimsky's own statement in *My Musical Life* that the Musorgsky original had been a success when it had first been produced. "Yes," said Toscanini, "but only in Russia."

The Metropolitan *Otello* reminded him of Tamagno and *Otello*. "I ask: 'You sing always so?' He say: 'Yes, I sing always so.' I ask Verdi, and is not true."

"To get Tamagno," he continued, "we must take Calvé in opera called *Messalina*. When she sing this opera for me composer play piano; and I ask him: 'You are satisfied?' He say: 'Yes, I am satisfied.' Calvé tell me when I may come to hotel for rehearsal; and I tell her we make rehearsal in theater. She leave the same day"; and he chuckled.

It must have been the discussion of *Boris Godunov* that reminded him of Chaliapin. "We ask him, but he will not sing at La Scala. After I am gone he sing there"—this with another chuckle. "He sing in first *Mefistofele*. When I hear him in *Mefistofele* later I would not speak to him. But later I hear him in first *Boris* in Paris, and I go to him and say I must embrace him."

And it may have been on this occasion that he told me

the story of his first orchestral concert in Turin, to show that "Toscanini was always Toscanini. I make rehearsal in pit; then I say I must have rehearsal on stage because in concert orchestra will play on stage. Manager say is not necessary; I say I will not conduct concert. This man was like father to me; but when is time for concert I am in bed. Manager come to hotel; but I stay in bed." And so the concert was given only after Toscanini had had his rehearsal on stage.

He remembered that I had written him about a photograph —one of him rehearsing with the Philadelphia Orchestra— which Mason Jones, the great first horn of the orchestra, had asked me to take to Toscanini to be autographed. I had brought it with me and gave it to Toscanini, who examined it closely, compared it with one on the piano, and then said: "E bella," which was true. He now addressed himself to what turned out to be the formidable operation of autographing it —which is to say that first he had to find the bottle of white ink, then the pen, and then he began to make stroke after stroke of the inscription with an intensity that was awesome, revealing, and moving.

I said there had always been a great mystery about his leaving the Metropolitan in 1915, and asked him if he would tell me why he left. "I could be millionaire," he said, "but I am somebody who could say no. In 1915 I find impossible to stay in Metropolitan: is no discipline. With me, yes; but with other conductors, no. I say to Gatti-Casazza: 'You need position; you stay. I do not need to stay; I go.' Later Otto Kahn come to me: 'Maestro, what I hear? Is impossible to believe you leave Metropolitan.' I say: 'When are performances of Un Ballo in Maschera and we must have five musicians to play on stage you say why we do not take five musicians from orchestra. I know: they tell me. In this theater I cannot work.' I go to Italy. In Milan I give concert for charity: I invite all musicians and singers for nothing; and Mr. Kahn send $1,000, but I do not answer him. For five years I conduct for charity and do not make a penny. After war they ask me to come back to La Scala. I do not want to go; but they say I must. I begin with five operas; next year twelve; and I conduct ninety performances in season. Then other conductors conduct more and more, and I conduct only fifty performances. Then I feel I cannot take responsibility for season, and I resign."

He described the system of rehearsal: the productions of the first year required only one or two rehearsals the second year; and rehearsal time went to the new productions. "At Metropolitan when I repeat *Götterdämmerung* second year I have only [two?] rehearsals."

Toscanini's reference to Mahler as "crazy man" is the last comment of his about another conductor that I recall; and with the record of my experience in this matter all in I will say what I have concluded about it. It has been alleged that Toscanini spoke only ill of other conductors, and that this was evidence of the jealousy that showed itself further in his treatment of some of the eminences who were associated with him —notably Stokowski, Bruno Walter, Mengelberg. But in my experience Toscanini did *not* speak only ill of other conductors: he spoke well of Ansermet, whose enormous success with the press and the public should on the contrary have aroused the jealousy attributed to him; he spoke with especial warmth of Schuch, the one-time director of the Dresden Opera; he spoke of Nikisch as a good conductor, but criticized him for his occasional insufficient study of the score and for the acting on the podium that others have told me Nikisch indulged in; similarly he spoke well of De Sabata but disapprovingly of his violent gesticulation. And here we come to the point of the matter: in my experience, whenever Toscanini spoke ill of a conductor he did so on the basis of something the conductor had done that seemed to Toscanini dreadfully, shockingly, intolerably wrong. With Muck and certain others it was their wrong tempos; with A— it was the achieving of excitement by whipping up tempo; with Koussevitzky it was the musical ignorance exemplified by, among other things, the failure to interpolate a cadenza where it was indicated in the score.

Concerning Stokowski and Walter at NBC I can report no statement by Toscanini; but in the spring of 1943 one of the serious musicians in the orchestra told me repeatedly about Stokowski's "line" of the moment, which was to exhort the orchestra not to be bound by the printed score, but instead to be creative, to improvise. This musician and others in the orchestra took Stokowski's "line" to be directed against Toscanini's principle of strict adherence to the printed score; and its consequence in practice was that the orchestra played with less than the absolute technical precision Toscanini demanded of it. For Toscanini, then, Stokowski was someone who not only advocated the violation of a principle Toscanini believed in, but, as a result, did not hold the orchestra to what Toscanini regarded as the proper technical standards.

Something of the same kind happened with Bruno Walter. In Salzburg in 1937 the American composer and conductor Hermann Hans Wetzler reported to me Toscanini's remark to him: "When Walter comes to something beautiful he melts. I suffer!" Nothing more perceptive was ever said about Walter; but it didn't keep Toscanini and Walter from being professionally associated for several seasons in Salzburg and from being warm personal friends, or keep Toscanini from inviting Walter to conduct the NBC Symphony. What ended all this, I was told at the time, was that during one of the periods when Walter was conducting the NBC Symphony in the broadcasts, Toscanini had to rehearse it for a concert in Newark, and was enraged by the technically unprecise playing, for which he held Walter responsible.

As for Mengelberg, his musical distortions and vulgarities must have been extremely distasteful to Toscanini; but his departure from the New York Philharmonic, I was told at the time, resulted from his talking against Toscanini to the orchestra, which caused Toscanini to request the Philharmonic to choose between Mengelberg and himself.

And as for Mahler, the Toscanini remark I have quoted must surely have had additional musical causes beside Mahler's treatment of the appoggiatura; but it also characterized Mahler as a person; and all accounts describe Mahler as a morbidly unhappy, tormented and "difficult" man, whose behavior might have seemed "crazy" to Toscanini.

When I visited Toscanini late in October 1949, I found him playing an NBC recording of a broadcast of the *Love Scene* from Berlioz's *Romeo and Juliet*. He was to broadcast the piece that week; also, Leonard Bernstein, who was going to conduct excerpts from *Romeo* that season, had come up the day before to ask Toscanini about his tempo in the Victor performance of the *Love Scene;* and they had compared the Victor *Love Scene* with the one from the 1947 broadcast of the entire work, and had found that the Victor was in fact faster. "I say is possible one day I am stupid," said Toscanini, who told me that in addition to playing the usual instrumental excerpts Bernstein was going to end with *Romeo in the Vault of the Capulets.* "I say is impossible to finish concert with *piano;* but he want to play this piece." And possibly it gave Toscanini the idea of playing it too; for a little later he said: "I will play all *Romeo and Juliet* next year again, because I am the only one who conduct this work." It was in this accidental way that works were suggested to him for performance; and it wasn't surprising, therefore, that in the end they weren't performed—as Berlioz's *Romeo* wasn't the following year.

Later in the fall Toscanini broadcast Beethoven's *Eroica* again, presumably in order that he might record it for Victor. All through 1948–49, someone at Victor told me, the company hadn't approached Toscanini about recording, having concerned itself with Horowitz, Heifetz, Rubinstein, Iturbi, Mario Lanza and other greats. And so some of the outstanding performances of that year—including the *Eroica* and Schubert *Unfinished* of the spring series—had not been recorded. This had led me, in May, to write a letter of protest to David Sarnoff, president of RCA, who had replied that the *Eroica* would be recorded before Toscanini's departure for Europe. Unfortunately Toscanini had then slipped in the bathtub, injuring his arm; and the recording sessions had therefore been canceled. And so it was in November that Victor recorded an *Eroica* of less intensity and power than the one of the preceding February, though impressively powerful considered by itself.

Still later there was a rehearsal of the Prelude to *Parsifal* which caused one of the men in the orchestra to exclaim afterward that nobody but Toscanini could have conducted the piece beating not the usual eight but a slow four to the measure—a subtly inflected four that was hair-raising in the sustained power with which it filled out the intervals of time with life and continuity in the flow of the sound. (In April 1954, at the first rehearsal for his tragic final broadcast, he would attempt something similar with the Prelude to *Lohengrin*, and not be able to bring it off.)

During a few rehearsals in the spring series, for the first and only times, I stood behind the percussion section in the passageway between the stage of Studio 8H and an unused control room, from where I could see Toscanini's face—attentive, alert, apprehensively watchful in all directions—as he marshaled the playing along. And observing him in operation in this way I noticed one thing more. I had been aware of the cohesive tension in the musical progression forward; now I became aware of the lateral tension which held the ninety-odd players in precisely right relation to each other, and the strands of continuing sound in the precise balance that produced the transparency of texture characteristic of his performances.

A few moments of one of these rehearsals that I had occasion to describe at the time may be of interest. Winthrop Sargeant, then a writer for *Life*, had described, in *Time-Life* style, how a rehearsal began: "Toscanini glances quickly over the assembled orchestra and, without further preamble, the baton descends like the knife of a guillotine." And Sargeant had also contended that Toscanini didn't use with an orchestra the explanatory technique of other conductors—that where they "will describe what they wish to obtain and the method to be pursued in achieving it, Toscanini will produce the effect . . . by setting up in the player's consciousness an emotional reaction which automatically produces it." Among the rehearsals I attended from 1942 on there were some at which Toscanini said good morning or afternoon, waited for the orchestra to become still and attentive, and "without further preamble" began to conduct. But more often I saw him do what he did on March 2, 1950, when, after his good morning, he picked up the score of Tchaikovsky's *Pathétique*, found the fourth measure after letter M in the third movement, explained to the flutes and clarinets that in this measure he wanted them to break off the held G-sharp in order to attack the subsequent descending scale with an accent, and had them

do this for him several times; then found the similar measure
at letter Z and had the strings and woodwinds play it in the
same way; then began to conduct the movement from the beginning, but stopped after the second measure because the
strings had not been precisely together, began again, stopped
again, and told the violas: "You make the bow jump too high,"
illustrating by bouncing his baton on his finger; then began
again and—the violas now being precisely together with the
violins—went on, but stopped after the third measure to tell
the oboes and bassoons they were not playing an accurate two
against the other woodwinds' three, and got this measure
played correctly; and so on thereafter. And I don't recall a rehearsal without its explanations and discussions with the first-
desk string-players of methods of bowing that would produce
the phrasing or accentuation or lack of accentuation Toscanini
wanted.[14]

A few weeks after this rehearsal of the *Pathétique* an amusing incident occurred during a rehearsal of the second movement of Debussy's *Ibéria*. In the eighth measure the horn
plays a motif which rises to D-sharp; two measures later the
cellos mutter the same motif, but with D-natural instead of
D-sharp; and on this occasion when the horn played the
D-sharp Toscanini stopped, told the player he should have
played D-natural, and began the movement again. This time
again the horn played D-sharp; and again Toscanini stopped
and told the player he should have played D-natural, and began the movement a third time. By now the atmosphere was
tense; and when the horn played D-sharp again I was prepared
for an explosion—instead of which Toscanini continued to conduct without a word: he had evidently remembered that it
was D-natural for the cellos but D-sharp for the horn.

The spring series ended with the performance, on April 1
and 8, of *Falstaff*. From the way Toscanini spoke of this opera

[14] But Marsh—on the basis of experience unknown to me—writes,
in *Toscanini and the Art of Orchestral Performance*, that unlike
Rodzinski, whose knowledge of English made him "able to analyze
difficulties and tell the men how to cope with them," Toscanini had
an orchestra "simply [play] for many minutes at a time, going over
works again and again until [he] was satisfied."

it seemed to be the one he cared about most; his performance of it had been one of his most famous achievements; and this one too was dazzlingly and enchantingly swift and light and clear. It is one of the performances in which some critics have reported hearing inexpressive singing that betrays the singers' inexperience in their parts and their terror of Toscanini; but listening to it again after a few years, when it was issued in Victor LM-6111, confirmed my original impression of the excellent singing of the entire cast except the tenor who sang Fenton, and made me freshly aware of the beauty and expressive inflection and coloring of Valdengo's singing, the powerful dramatic projection of Cloe Elmo, the technical and musical security of Teresa Stich-Randall's use of her exquisite lyric soprano. It was possible to argue that a weightier voice than Valdengo's would have been even better for Falstaff, and a less youthful one than Guarerra's better for Ford; but not to say, as one critic did, that the performance was accurate but had very little more to recommend it.

And *Falstaff* was followed by the transcontinental tour which began with the concert in New York's Carnegie Hall on April 14 and ended with the one in Philadelphia's Academy of Music on May 27. During this season the years of work under Toscanini had begun to be audible in the orchestra's playing, as the men themselves realized: "You know," I heard one of them exclaim, "we're beginning to sound like a symphony orchestra!" And the truth of this statement was demonstrated right at the start of the New York concert—in the performance of Rossini's Overture to *L'Italiana in Algeri*, which had a precision and finish, a refinement of tone and subtlety of nuance, a sensitiveness to Toscanini's direction, that made it possible to think one was hearing the Philharmonic in 1936. However the performances at this concert—including the Beethoven *Eroica* and Debussy *La Mer*—didn't reach the heights of the ones at later concerts, after the weeks in which Toscanini and the orchestra continued to rehearse and play the works they had prepared for the tour. I was told of an especially wonderful *Eroica* in Pasadena; and at the final concert in Philadelphia I heard a *La Mer* that was phenomenal as a realization of the piece, as an exhibition of virtuoso or-

chestral performance, and in the relaxed ease with which conductor and orchestra operated. The NBC Symphony had
become one of the world's great orchestras; and it remained
that to the end.

That year a collection of my *Nation* articles had been published under the title *Music in the Nation*; and when a copy
was sent to Toscanini I wrote him that he was to consider
this book too as dedicated to him. I had a telephone call from
him, in the course of which he said he had been reading the
book: "What you say about me is too much. But why is not
inscribed?" I explained that the copy he had received had
come from the publisher, and that I was inscribing to him a
special leather-bound copy which the publisher had given me.
And when I sent it to him I said I had been thinking of what
he might do now with the first copy of the trade edition, and
it had occurred to me that he might inscribe it to me.

I didn't see him that spring until the day he was to leave
on the tour, which I believe was Easter Sunday. I had volun-
teered to Walter Toscanini to put into order, while his father
was away, the 16-inch acetate records of the NBC broadcasts,
some of which were in a closet next to Toscanini's study, and
the rest piled high in complete disorder everywhere in the
room. And on this Sunday morning I went up to discuss with
Walter how the job was to be done. While I was talking to
him and to the secretary, Miss Eugenia Gale, in the study,
Toscanini appeared—not in his usual sober black, but very
natty in light gray trousers, gray shirt, and tan shoes with gray
cloth tops.

"Did you hear *Falstaff*?" he asked, his face lighting up.

"Yes, it was very beautiful," I answered.

"Ah," he said, "for me is *most* beautiful opera!"

At this moment a messenger delivered a parcel of test pressings on which Victor wanted his approval before he left. "Yes,"
said Toscanini, "I want to hear. Find G-minor: I want to hear
finale." Walter found the record and began to play it; but Toscanini interrupted: "They change machine; *allóra* is different
sound and I cannot hear." So we moved to his bedroom, which
now had the equipment he was accustomed to. The room was

in a state of great disorder and commotion with preparations for the trip; nevertheless the record was played; and as we stood listening I noticed the two copies of my book on a table. After the finale Toscanini asked for another record of the G-minor, which couldn't be found; then he remembered wanting to hear the first movement of Schubert's *Unfinished,* "because first time oboe play too loud: must be *piano* and is *forte.*" The record was found and played; Toscanini stood conducting and listening intently, and pointed as the oboe began its first statement *forte;* and when the oboe played the repetition of the statement *piano* he pointed again and said: "So is correct—*piano.* I want to hear second time"—meaning the second take, which couldn't be found.

The playing of test pressings ended, Walter and I returned to the study to resume our discussion of what to do with the NBC records. After a short time Toscanini reappeared, holding in his hand the first copy of my book. Handing it to me with a trace of a smile, but saying nothing, he again left the room. And when I opened the book to the first blank page I saw that he had originally written his name diagonally across it, and had now added below his name an inscription to the author of the book who, he wrote, had made him blush many times as he had read it.

I saw Toscanini again a few days after the final concert of the tour in Philadelphia. I had written him enthusiastically about the *La Mer,* and had reproached him for the terrible thing he had done to me by playing Brahms's First in place of the Fourth that had been announced. And I went up to Riverdale to report to Walter Toscanini what had been accomplished with the NBC records. I hadn't been able to complete the job, and continued with it after Toscanini left for Italy; and I found not only some of the wartime glass-based acetates broken, but a large number of records in varying states of deterioration caused by the sulphuric acid in the paper of the envelopes. It was this deterioration that led Walter Toscanini to transfer all his father's recordings from disc to tape; and unfortunately the first Victor engineer who did the work for him had ideas about beefing up Toscanini's Vic-

tor recordings with echo chamber and peaking of treble, and
seems to have been able to persuade Toscanini to substitute
his in some instances monstrously falsified "enhanced" versions for the originals.

When I walked into the office on the top floor I found Miss
Gale and a man checking the names on the photographs
(amusing ones of Toscanini seated in the ski lift at Sun Valley)
that Toscanini had inscribed to the members of the orchestra
in remembrance of the tour. As I stood talking to Walter
Toscanini his father entered the room, and with barely a nod
to the visitor whom his nearsighted eyes didn't recognize he
addressed himself to Miss Gale. But at that moment he heard
and recognized my voice; and with a smile he came over to
shake hands with me.

"I will tell you why I play Brahms First in Philadelphia.
Somebody ask for Brahms Fourth in Washington; *allóra* I play
First in Philadelphia. But why you do not like First? Is beautiful music. Of course Fourth is better—finale has wonderful
harmony [I think that by 'harmony' Toscanini meant writing
for winds]. But First is beautiful too. You write once—a word
—'bombastic'! But no-o-o!" I said it was the first movement
that I found bombastic. "Oh no-o-o! Is beautiful!" And the
second movement I found excessively sentimental. "Oh no-o-o!
When is played too slow, yes; but in right tempo is beautiful!
And Third Symphony——" I said I didn't like the third movement of this one. "Oh no-o-o! In right tempo is beautiful!"
And he demonstrated by singing it to me, as everyone in the
room grinned.

"Brahms's symphonies," Toscanini went on, "are first after
Beethoven. Schumann? You like Fourth, but——" and he caricatured the principal theme of the first movement. I reminded
him of the slow movement. "Yes, is beautiful, but——" and
again he caricatured the first movement. "I play only one
symphony of Schumann, the—the——" "The Third?" I suggested. "Yes, the Third. And Second has beautiful Andante,
but——" and he caricatured the first movement. "Schumann:
no! Schubert? Is not like Mozart, who write too easy—without
work. (Beethoven: you can hear how he worked!) But no
harmony." [One would suppose he said Schubert *was* like

Mozart in the ease of his writing; but I have given what my notes have. His thought on Schubert isn't clear, especially from a man who played the C-major Symphony at his very first orchestral concert and so many times thereafter.] Mendelssohn? No. *Italian* Symphony? I object as Italian to saltarello finale. When I play cello I play once in E-flat Quartet, and I hear is weak: I never play Mendelssohn again—until I hear movement with theme like *Parsifal*——" "The *Reformation* Symphony?" "Yes, *Reformation* Symphony."

Later, "Tonight I record *La Mer*. And tomorrow Brahms Fourth, because in Washington orchestra play beautifully, and I think this performance should be recorded." "Yes," I said, "but the performance of *Ibéria* is more important to record." "Ye-e-es; but I want to record Brahms Fourth because orchestra play so beautifully." "Yes," I persisted, "but *Ibéria*." He also persisted; and this impasse too was not resolved.

"After tour," he said, "I am not tired. But for one broadcast I am tired. Three rehearsals and one broadcast I am more tired as six weeks of tour." This led to a discussion of the reason I mentioned earlier in this book: the tension of the first public performance at the broadcast, as against the relaxed feeling with the repetitions after a first performance.

At this point Miss Gale told him he would have to inscribe three more photographs, and gave him the names. With a rueful smile he said: "After writing so much I *am* tired." I said I had brought along a photograph which I liked especially, and I wondered whether he would agree. He watched with interest as I extracted from the envelope a photograph of him at a rehearsal, demonstrating something to the cellists, with his left hand holding his baton as though it were a cello and his right hand holding an imaginary bow. "Oh ye-e-es," he said. "I remember this. Where is it?" "It must be either Vienna or Salzburg," I said. "Yes, Vienna or Salzburg." "I wonder if you would be kind enough to sign it for me." He didn't answer but merely took the photograph from me and left the room. I resumed my conversation with Walter; and after some time Toscanini reappeared, holding the photograph in his hand and exclaiming: "I look everywhere—in letters—in books—in telephone book—everywhere, but I cannot find your first name!" So he had inscribed it to B. H. Haggin.

Again he left the room; and a little later he reappeared with a paper which he gave to Miss Gale and discussed with her briefly. Then, as he turned from her he said with a smile and a shrug: "I am supposed to have bad character." Another shrug: "Is not true—but they say." And he left.

That night I went to the recording session in Studio 8H. This was the first reassembling of the orchestra since the tour; and so there was a happy atmosphere in the place and much excited talk. The performance of La Mer that was recorded was the phenomenal one I had heard in Philadelphia a few days before, but with its sound in the Academy of Music now altered in Studio 8H. I didn't stay for the recording of Saint-Saëns's Danse Macabre, but went again the next night for the recording of Brahms's Fourth, and was dumbfounded when I was told that not Brahms's Fourth was to be recorded—but Debussy's Ibéria!

When the first movement had been recorded a break was announced for playback. There was a delay; and Toscanini left the studio, while the men of the orchestra drifted off the stage and stood around on the floor in groups. Then the play-back began; and it had proceeded for only a few measures when Toscanini came rushing into the studio in great agitation, gesticulating with his right arm in protest, and exclaiming: "Is wrong tempo! Machine play too slow!" Actually he had played the movement in a delightfully lilting tempo which—I was assured by members of the orchestra—was the one in which he had played it the several times on the tour; but listening from the outside of the performance, so to speak, he had now found it too slow. The orchestra was quickly reassembled and rehearsed in a faster tempo; the movement was then recorded a second time; and this performance satisfied him. And the intense feeling about playing too slowly continued—not only for the recording of the rest of Ibéria, but for the remaking of the first movement of Schubert's Unfinished.

My meeting with Toscanini the day before left me with every reason to suppose I would see him again in the fall; but my letters the next year brought no answering telephone call or invitation to visit him, and for reasons that remained undisclosed to me I never had an opportunity to speak to him again. There was the possibility that something I wrote angered him; but this seemed improbable when I received one of the Christmas cards he sent out from Italy the year after his retirement. On one page was a photograph of Toscanini looking at an opened score with a photograph of Verdi nearby, and reproduced underneath this the theme of the closing fugue of *Falstaff* with the words *Tutto nel mondo è burla l'uom è* copied by Toscanini; and reproduced on the opposite page was his handwritten Christmas and New Year greeting, signature and date.

ADDENDA

2

REHEARSALS AND PERFORMANCES
OF THE LAST YEARS

Though I had no further meetings with Toscanini I continued to attend rehearsals. He was inactive in the fall of 1950, for reasons which were at first reported to be anger at the transfer of the broadcasts from Studio 8H (which NBC had converted into a television studio) to Carnegie Hall, and from Saturday at six-thirty to Monday at ten, and which were later reported to be trouble with a knee. I cannot say whether these reports were correct; but I can say why they were believable. The men of the orchestra told me they hated Studio 8H because they couldn't hear each other; and one of the pleasures of the tour had been the experiences of playing in several fine auditoriums in which they said they had heard details in performances that they had never heard before. But Toscanini, they said, liked Studio 8H because standing on the podium *he* could hear everything very clearly. In addition, I was told, he felt that just as Carnegie Hall was the Philharmonic's place, 8H was *his* place; and I remember hearing about recording sessions scheduled for Carnegie Hall which at the last minute he insisted on transferring to 8H. These were the reasons I knew about that may have caused him to object to the move to Carnegie Hall, which one would have expected him to welcome since it was so good for the broadcasts. Monday at ten also was better for them than Saturday at six-thirty: it was a time when music-lovers were free to listen not only in the East but in other parts of the country where it was nine and eight (if, that is, the broadcasts were carried live). But we have seen that when NBC sold the Sunday-at-five spot it convinced Toscanini that more people listened Saturday at six-thirty; and he now insisted on NBC's moving the broadcasts back to that time. As for the knee trouble, there was visible evidence of it when he did resume conducting—in the fact that his left hand frequently grasped the railing around the podium, presumably to relieve the strain on the left knee.

Toscanini may have been unhappy in Carnegie Hall, but for the orchestra and the listener the place was a pleasure. I retain in my memory the beautiful sound of Beethoven's Fourth at the rehearsals for the performance of February 3, 1951—in particular the silken, luminous sound of the violins; and my reason for remembering it is that on this occasion the performance had to be broadcast from a tape which transmitted a muffled falsification of the sound I had heard, and which was the source of the recording later issued by Victor.

I remember also certain rehearsals in the fall. Toscanini returned from Italy with his knee trouble gone, his powers operating with amazing energy; and the virtuosity of the orchestra and its sensitiveness to his direction made possible an almost casual achievement of the magic that is so difficult to achieve in Berlioz's *Queen Mab*. They also made it possible for even first readings to exhibit the precision and tonal beauty that I remember hearing at the first rehearsal of Dvořák's Symphonic Variations; and at the first rehearsal of the Prelude to Act 3 of *Die Meistersinger* the integrated sound of the brass section, plastically shaped and sensitively inflected like the sound of one instrument, took my breath away.

And yet when the performance of Rossini's *Semiramide* Overture recorded by Victor in the fall of 1951 was issued a few years later and was compared with the 1936 Philharmonic performance, it was astonishing to hear the NBC Symphony's playing—seemingly unsurpassable—surpassed right at the start, in the slow introduction, by the subtleties of attack, inflection and coloring of the Philharmonic horns, and later, in the Allegro, by the energy of the Philharmonic violins in their soft opening statements, the sensitized response of the full orchestra. Nor was this all. Nothing, seemingly, could be more effective than the pacing and shaping of the piece in the

1951 performance; and so it was astonishing to hear how much more effective the Philharmonic performance of the introduction was with its relaxed expansiveness involving great elasticity of tempo, than the NBC Symphony performance with its faster, tighter simplicity involving only slight modifications of tempo. But the most striking and significant difference occurred at the point in the Allegro where the long concluding crescendo of the exposition breaks off for the series of violin statements leading to the recapitulation: in the 1951 performance these violin statements were inflected not only without the breadth but without the force and sustained tension they had in the 1936 performance, revealing once again the lessened energy that had manifested itself a couple of times before—in the V-J Day *Eroica* when it was compared with the 1944 performance; in the 1948 Strauss *Don Quixote* when it was compared with the 1938 performance. And let me emphasize that such occasional lessened powers and effectiveness in the later years were something one became aware of only when the performance was compared with an earlier one. If one listened to the 1951 Verdi *Requiem* or the 1953 Beethoven *Missa Solemnis* without comparing it with the 1940 *Requiem* or *Missa*, one was aware only of phenomenal powers operating to produce a performance that was wonderfully right, effective and beautiful, and playing by the orchestra that was something to marvel at.

Nor did the later performance always reveal lessened powers and effectiveness when compared with the earlier ones: the opposite also happened on occasion, as the performance of the *Tristan* Prelude and Finale that Toscanini recorded early in 1952 demonstrates. For more than thirty years we have been able to get an idea of the Toscanini *Tristan* that Carl Van Vechten called overwhelming only from Toscanini's performances of the Prelude and Finale. I recall that the performance of these two excerpts was in fact overwhelming the first time in 1926; it was overwhelming each of the numerous times thereafter; and most overwhelming, it seems to me, is the performance that comes off LM-6020. For comparison of this performance with earlier ones preserved on records reveals that the performance changed in the course of time, and that the change was of an unusual kind: whereas tempos generally tended to become faster in Toscanini's later performances, in the *Tristan* Prelude and Finale they became much slower, giving the music increased expressive force. I retained from the first performance in 1926 a recollection of a marked and exciting acceleration in the Prelude soon after the direction *Belebend* in the score; and this is confirmed by the records with the performance broadcast in 1938, the one recorded in 1942, the one at the Red Cross concert in 1944: in these performances the Prelude, after the introductory statements, proceeds with great slowness and weight, with powerful inflection and tension of phrase, with tremendous expressive force, until in the eleventh measure after *Belebend* it begins to accelerate rapidly to a much faster tempo in which it continues thereafter in exciting fashion, broadening out momentarily for the climax of the *meno forte* passage, then resuming its rapid course in the final crescendo, and broadening out again in the last two measures of this crescendo for the climax of the piece. But in 1952 the acceleration after *Bèlebend* is slight, so that the piece continues with slowness, breadth and powerful inflection—which is to say with more powerful expressive effect than in 1938—broadening out tremendously at the climax of the *meno forte* passage, then resuming its slow and powerful course in the final crescendo, and broadening out even more tremendously for the climax of the piece. And the 1952 Finale also is enormously slower than the one of 1938—with, consequently, more breadth and power, and with increased expressive effect of exaltation and transfiguration.

These changes—and others concerned with smaller details—are not only fascinating in themselves but moving in what they tell us about Toscanini. The *Tristan* piece was one of those Toscanini played most; but even after many performances his mind continued to work at it, to change it for increased esthetic and expressive effect; and the next performance, down to the last, was not a perfunctory routine act but a fresh application of attention and energy.[1]

[1] But Marsh, in *Toscanini and the Art of Orchestral Performance*, writes concerning the *Tristan* performance in LM-6020: "In Alma Mah-

Fascinating and moving in the same ways are the changes in the great performance of Schubert's C-major early in 1953, recorded on LM-1835—the changes one discovers when one compares it with the great performance with the Philadelphia Orchestra in 1941. Toscanini played this work at his very first orchestral concert in 1896; and one would think that by 1941 his mind had achieved finality about it. But the changes in 1953 make it clear that he had continued to think about it, and in this thought to be concerned with an esthetic end—the esthetic beauty, for him, of a movement played in a single tempo with only slight modifications that are the more effective for the steadiness from which they depart. This single tempo in the Allegro of the first movement is—again in surprising reversal of his tendency toward faster tempos in later years—slower in 1953 than in 1941, and is accelerated only a little in the *Più moto* coda, which means that it has to slow down only a little for the concluding proclamations of the theme of the introduction. But for this satisfaction Toscanini sacrifices the greater momentum created by the faster 1941 tempo in the Allegro, and especially by its greater acceleration in the coda, where from measure 589 the canonic series of overlapping statements of winds, then violins, then low

---

ler's biography of her husband, we learn of Mahler's misgivings about Toscanini's performances of *Tristan* . . . I share Mahler's reservations. The performance (there is no reason to believe it has changed in the intervening years) is over-refined, the antiseptic souvenir of passion rather than its full-blooded actuality. In *Tristan* this will not do, although it is easily understood when we see that these two works rank fourth and fifth in frequency in Toscanini's repertory: they have had all the life played out of them." But Marsh, intent on associating himself with Mahler, pays too little attention to what Alma Mahler actually says about the Toscanini *Tristan* of 1909—that "the nuances in his Wagner were distressing. His style has been simplified since those days"; and he therefore doesn't perceive that in his disapproval of the "over-refined . . . antiseptic" Toscanini *Tristan* which he had invented he is not sharing *her* disapproval of the nuanced Toscanini *Tristan* she reports having heard in 1909, and is instead disagreeing with her evident approval of what she describes as Toscanini's simplified later style in Wagner. Nor does Marsh perceive that the disapproval she reports is her own, not her husband's; and as it happens, Bruno Walter, a more truthful witness than Alma, reported Mahler's telling him, after hearing Toscanini's *Tristan*, that although it was different from theirs it was very beautiful.

strings are bound together by the fast tempo into a single large-spanned utterance that is tremendously exciting. On the other hand, the single steady tempo in the finale is faster in 1953 than in 1941, with only a slight acceleration therefore in the coda, and only a slight broadening in the groups of four *sfz* unison C's. Thus the movement has all the momentum it has to have; but on the other hand the slightly more relaxed tempo in 1941 accelerates more in the coda, only to take one's breath away with the enormous slowing down and distention of the four unison C's, which creates each time a hair-raising tension that is released in the answering tutti in fast tempo again. Listening to the two performances one may decide that the earlier one was even greater than the later one; but one cannot fail to recognize that the later one was in its own way one of Toscanini's greatest.

And in the fall of 1953 there were other great performances —the wonderfully clarified Strauss *Don Quixote*, Berlioz *Harold in Italy* and Beethoven *Eroica*, and a Beethoven *Coriolan* Overture with breadth and distentions that gave it a power beyond any I recalled. I heard the rehearsals of *Don Quixote*, and still remember the orchestra's great first cellist, Frank Miller, seated out in front, grunting audibly (in the empty hall) with the effort of his huge body that produced playing extraordinary in its elegance of style as well as the tensile strength of its tone and the cohesive tension of its phrasing. But these rehearsals were my last: a letter from Walter Toscanini regretted having to inform me that nobody was to be allowed henceforth at the Thursday afternoon and Friday morning rehearsals, but that I would be on the list of guests invited to the Saturday afternoon dress rehearsal (the broadcasts had been moved to Sunday at six-thirty). He didn't say why; and it was not until late in the season that events suggested what the reason may have been.

After an interval of four years there was again, on January 17 and 24, 1954, a performance of an opera—Verdi's *Un Ballo in Maschera*. Concerning this it was no less considerable a critic than Virgil Thomson who wrote that the "almost circus-like showmanship" of the orchestra performance had made demands of volume and bravura which the singers had been unable to meet, with the result that in Carnegie Hall "they were pretty thoroughly overpowered" and "were obliged so consistently to force their volume that much of the singing I did hear was both ugly in sound and only approximate in pitch." I was in Carnegie Hall too, and can testify that in some of the climaxes the singers *were* overpowered by the orchestral tuttis that have overpowered the singers in every performance everywhere, but that in the more lightly scored passages at other times—which is to say most of the time—the orchestral accompaniment was beautifully adjusted to the singing, whose every *piano* reached me at the back of the hall without the slightest forcing. If there were occasional unlovely vocal sounds and deviations from pitch it was because Robert Merrill's baritone had become rough and coarse and Herva Nelli simply didn't always sing squarely on pitch.

This review, I might add, was typical of Thomson's performances with Toscanini. He was a brilliantly perceptive critic when his mind operated on the real facts before him; but there were occasions when it was concerned not with real facts but with others that existed only in his head, and when he applied to them general ideas with no more basis in reality; and Toscanini's performances were such occasions. It is anyone's privilege not to like a Toscanini performance; but the performance and the reasons for disliking it must be real. When some Germans objected to the luminous clarity and grace of Toscanini's *Meistersinger* or his Brahms as being unsuitable for music they contended called rather for breadth and solidity, they were applying understandable and valid criteria to correctly heard performances. But what Thomson did for almost fifteen years was to apply imaginary ideas to imaginary Toscanini performances. The *Ballo in Maschera* he objected to was largely imaginary; and an example of imaginary ideas was the business of the marriage of historical and literary with musical culture in the Great Tradition of Wagner, Von Bülow, Nikisch and Beecham that, according to Thomson, was lacking in Toscanini's conducting, but that I suspect was lacking also in Wagner's, Von Bülow's, Nikisch's and Beecham's. Toscanini's actual style of performance, which gave a piece of music plastically coherent shape, Thomson described with the term 'streamlining,' which was incorrect; and this term was part of numerous schematizations by pure invention—e.g., "when one memorizes everything, one acquires a great awareness of music's run-through. One runs it through in the mind constantly; and one finds in that way a streamlined rendering that is wholly independent of detail and even of specific significance, a disembodied version that is all shape and no texture. Later, in rehearsal, one returns to texture; and one takes care that it serve always as neutral surfacing for the shape. But shape is what any piece is always about that one has memorized through the eye and the inner ear." Actually, Toscanini away from the podium did not keep running through pieces of music in his mind, but kept reading them in the score, and in this constant study of the printed score was concerned always with texture—i.e., with this bassoon part or that viola part buried in the tutti that must be made clearly audible in the performance.

What Thomson started, others continued: I was told of one insignificant young commentator on the radio whose way of making himself appear big was to talk about Toscanini's lack of culture. The writing about Toscanini was always one of the forms of exploitation of him: formerly the way to show one's understanding was to praise him, today it is to find fault with him; and the attacks reveal as little understanding of the Toscanini operation and what it produced as did most of the praise.

It was interesting, one Sunday afternoon in March 1954, to listen to the broadcast of Cantelli's performance with the New York Philharmonic of the Mozart Divertimento K.287 that Toscanini had played, and to listen later in the day to the broadcast of Toscanini's performances of Verdi's *Te Deum* and Vivaldi's Concerto Grosso No. 11 from *L'Estro Armonico*. For the two broadcasts threw into sharp relief the difference between the two conductors. The relaxed flow in the fast movements of the Mozart piece had lyricism and grace, as against the powerful impulse that had operated in Toscanini's treatment of them; and to the Adagio also, which Cantelli made a beautifully shaped and eloquent vocal aria, Toscanini's power had imparted a largeness of span, a tension, a grandeur that had made its expressive effect overwhelming. And that power, creating a continuous tension in the flow of sound, and doing this in the quietest music no less than in the most forceful, was impressively evident in the lovely slow movement of the Vivaldi concerto no less than in the Allegros and in the *Te Deum.*

One heard the power being exercised in those pieces on that Sunday—exercised to hold the members of the orchestra in precisely balanced relation to one another, and to keep every sound in the progression in coherent relation to the next. But the next Sunday one heard that the power was *not* being exercised in the performance of Tchaikovsky's *Pathétique,* in which there was no continuity of impetus and tension, and one sound was not in coherent relation to the next. When I asked a musician in the orchestra about this he confirmed my impression: "He was all there in the rehearsal, but not in the performance." And so there was this to prepare me for what happened at the first rehearsal for the final broadcast on April 4.

I heard all three rehearsals as they came over a line from Carnegie Hall. At the first one, on Thursday afternoon, Toscanini began with the Prelude to *Lohengrin,* and announced: "I will conduct *alla breve*"—meaning a slow two to the measure instead of the usual four. It will be recalled that he had done something similar in the Prelude to *Parsifal* four years earlier, beating instead of the usual eight to the measure a slow four with sustained power that had filled out the intervals of time in exciting fashion. A member of the orchestra had exclaimed on that occasion that nobody but Toscanini could have done this; but now at the rehearsal of the *Lohengrin* Prelude it became evident that even Toscanini no longer could do it: after a few measures there was discord and confusion, the playing stopped, and I heard an apprehensive murmur go through the orchestra. "I conduct *alla breve,*" Toscanini repeated; and again the performance broke down in discord and confusion after a few measures, and I heard the murmur go through the orchestra. This time, as I recall it, Toscanini first demonstrated by singing the music as he beat time, then began again to conduct, but stopped to tell the violins to play the opening A-major chords without vibrato, which he said was suitable for *Inferno* but not for *Paradiso*. And I think the next time he began he was able to keep the performance going to the end.

When, some time later, I asked a musician in the orchestra about the breakdowns, he explained: "He didn't beat a two-to-the-measure that we could follow; and he himself began to follow our playing in four to the measure—which threw us off completely." Nor was this incident the only one of its kind that season. And so it suggested a possible reason for the decision not to allow anyone at rehearsals.

The *Lohengrin* Prelude was followed by the Prelude to *Die Meistersinger*; and I remember my surprise that Toscanini did nothing about the nerveless, poor playing. Then *Dawn and Rhine Journey* from *Die Götterdämmerung*, in which there were several stops for corrections that I don't remember, and one stop for something that was to have great importance two days later. The place was the entrance of the kettledrum in the passage immediately after the off-stage horn calls; and Toscanini contended that the timpanist had come in too soon. "It's the same part I always play," said the timpanist. "Maybe," said Toscanini. "All right, I'm always——" I didn't catch the timpanist's last word but presumed it was "wrong." Eventually the passage was played in the way Toscanini considered correct, and the piece was completed.

My notes for the rehearsal on Friday morning have "power all there" next to the Overture and Bacchanale of *Tannhäuser*, and again next to the *Götterdämmerung* piece; and that suffices to describe the different playing I heard that morning. There was one stop in the *Rhine Journey*, but not at the point where the trouble with the kettledrum had occurred the day before.

And so we come to Saturday afternoon's dramatic dress rehearsal. Power was all there again in the performances of the *Lohengrin* Prelude, the *Forest Murmurs* from *Siegfried*, and the *Götterdämmerung* piece as far as Toscanini got in it. My notes record his stopping at one point in the *Dawn* portion and shouting: "Staccato! Staccato! *Ignoranti, tutti!*" And they record his stopping in a fury at the point where the trouble with the kettledrum had occurred two days before. While Toscanini raged I heard Frank Miller call out to the timpanist: "Make it thirteen measures' rest instead of twelve." Twelve was right, and the timpanist had waited that number of measures; but Toscanini mistakenly thought it should be one more; and Miller was telling the timpanist to do what would seem right to Toscanini. "*È vergógna! Vergógna!*"[2] he shouted. And when the passage was repeated, as he thought, correctly, he stopped again and exclaimed: "*Finalmente!*" Then, in bitter anger: "*L'ultima prova!*"[3] There were long moments of silence; then I heard a murmur in the orchestra which told me something had happened; and when it swelled into conversation I realized that Toscanini was no longer on the podium. I heard a voice from a loud-speaker in Carnegie Hall announce the end of the rehearsal and ask the audience to leave but instruct the orchestra to remain on the stage. Time passed; then I heard the voice from the speaker again, this time dismissing the orchestra. The rehearsal was not completed.

To my ears, as I listened to the broadcast the next day, power was not exercised in the performances of the *Lohengrin* Prelude, the *Siegfried* excerpt, the *Götterdämmerung* piece, and the *Tannhäuser* Overture and Bacchanale. Nevertheless, when the climax of the Bacchanale had subsided into the quiet concluding section, I was unprepared for the shock of hearing the discordant evidence of instruments making wrong entrances. It lasted only a couple of moments; but it created an apprehensiveness about what was happening in Carnegie Hall; and these fears were seemingly confirmed when the performance suddenly was cut off, the voice of Ben Grauer announced that "technical difficulties" had necessitated an interruption of the broadcast, and a recorded performance of Brahms's First Symphony came over the air. I had witnessed the inconceivable: a Toscanini performance that had broken down. But suddenly the Brahms stopped and I was hearing

2 "It's a shame! A shame!"
3 "The last rehearsal!"

the conclusion of the Bacchanale, which apparently had *not* broken down. The piece ended, was applauded, and was followed by a nerveless playing of the notes of the *Meistersinger* Prelude, which concluded the broadcast.

From musicians in the orchestra I learned some of the things that had happened in Carnegie Hall. As early as the *Forest Murmurs* Toscanini had failed to beat a couple of changes of time signature, but with no bad consequences because the orchestra had played correctly. In the Bacchanale, when the orchestra had become aware that he was no longer conducting—his face showing his mind not to be in contact with the performance, his right arm gradually dropping to his side, his left hand covering his eyes—it had managed to keep going past the few wrong entrances, playing correctly after that; and Toscanini had begun to beat time again. Then, in the *Meistersinger* Prelude he had seemed to summon all his strength in the grim determination to beat time through the piece; and he had accomplished this, but not the conducting of a musical performance. (Actually he did not beat time to the very end of the piece, but was already off the podium when the orchestra was playing the final chords.) And through other sources it became known that when Toscanini had stopped conducting in the Bacchanale, Cantelli, in the control booth, had lost his head and insisted on the performance being taken off the air.

It seemed clear that at this tragic broadcast Toscanini had suffered a recurrence of the failing of his powers that had manifested itself now and then during that season. But it is possible that the failing this time was caused by the emotional strain he was under, which may also have been responsible for the happenings at the dress rehearsal the day before. One source of the strain was of course the fact that this was the end—the last rehearsal, the last broadcast; another was the heart attack suffered by Mrs. Walter Toscanini, whom Toscanini was very fond of. Emotional strain, or lessened strength, or both were evident in the signature—formerly sharply energetic, now wavering, blurred, unclear—on his letter of resignation, which NBC sent out in facsimile with David Sarnoff's reply. It was reported that throughout the day of the broadcast Toscanini had been undecided whether to conduct the concert; and it would have been better if he had not conducted it.

Two eyewitnesses have given different and astonishingly incorrect accounts of the happenings of those last two days. Vincent Sheean, in *First and Last Love* (Random House, 1956), has it that Toscanini at the broadcast broke down at precisely the point in the Bacchanale at which he had ended the rehearsal the day before—when in fact he didn't conduct the Bacchanale at all at the dress rehearsal. And Chotzinoff, in *Toscanini: An Intimate Portrait*, writes concerning the performance of the Bacchanale that the anxieties Toscanini had aroused before the broadcast were "routed" by what he observed from the control room—"the powerful gyrations of his baton, the mystic behavior of his left hand, and the subtle conspiratorial expressions of his eyes and lips." But then, says Chotzinoff, Toscanini faltered, and the orchestra "tried desperately to coalesce and reach the end in unity . . . The attempt, beset by self-consciousness and fear, was a failure. In the soft cacophony that ensued, the Maestro ceased conducting and put his hand to his eyes. The men stopped playing and the house was engulfed in terrible silence . . ." The facts are that the orchestra continued to play and succeeded in finishing the Bacchanale, after which the hall was filled by the audience's applause.

(I should add that this is not Chotzinoff's only invention in the book; and that his fluent lying is not its only objectionable feature. See the appendix containing the article *Genius Betrayed.*)

Two moments of a rehearsal with the NBC Symphony

"Once he started the progression going, he marshaled it along, watched over it, controlled it to make it come out as planned. The marshaling was done with those large, plastic, sensitive movements of his right arm (extended to the point of his baton), which delineated for the orchestra the flow of sound in much of its subtly inflected detail and literally conducted the orchestra from one sound to the next . . . The left hand meanwhile was in constant activity as the instrument of the apprehensive watchfulness that showed itself on Toscanini's face—now exhorting, now quieting, now warning, now suppressing."

The texts of the two letters on the following pages:

November 3—1941

My dear Mr Haggin
Yes, it will be one of my first records Schubert's C major
Symphony which I am going to conduct next week with the
Philadelphia Orchestra . . .
Also the Tchaikovsky Pathetic and Iberia and Reine Mab, too.
I have a weakness for Beethoven's Septet which I performed
last season with the N. B. C orchestra with ten violins, ten
violas—eight celli—and four basses—because I never
liked and enjoyed this wonderful music with the seven
instruments as it is written by Beethoven . . . I heard many
performances of this Septet in the original form and played by
distinguished musicians but the balance was never attained. I
shall read what you say about Schubert—Haydn—Mozart with
the utmost interest.
And about Brahms? For the moment "acqua in bocca" as the
italian proverb says. Cordial greetings from
                                    Arturo Toscanini

November 3—1944

My dear Haggin . . .
    Yes! you were right—you guessed my feeling—The
dedication to me of your last book on its front page would
have not been so dear to me as it is now that I know the
dedication comes silently from your own mind and heart—and
from the bottom of my heart comes to you my best thanks.
    And you wanted to add: "in recognition of what I owe
you" as a complement of the dedication! Dio mio!! You make
me blush as I blushed to day hearing the record of the Eroica
made a few years ago, pur troppo!
    When shall I have the pleasure to see you at Riverdale? I
hope soon—may be next week . . . I want very badly to ask you
something about your book . . .
    With my best good wishes very cordially
                                    Arturo Toscanini

November 3 - 1941

My dear Mr Hoffin

Yes, it will be one
of my first records
Schubert's C major symphony
which I am going to con
duct next week with the
Philadelphia Orchestra ...
Also the Tchaikovsky Pa-
thetic and Iberia and
Heine Werke too.
I have a weakness for

Beethoven's Septett which
I performed last season
with the N-B-C or-
chestra with ten violins,
ten violas - eight celli - and
four basses - because I
never liked and enjoyed
this wonderful music
with the seven instrument
as it is written by Beethoven ... I heard many
performances of this
Septett in the original
form and played by

November 3 - 1944

My dear Happie ...

Yes! you were right —
you guessed my feelings —
the dedication to me of
your last book on its front
pages would have not been
so dear to me as it is, you
that I know the dedication
comes silently from your own
mind and heart — and from
the bottom of my heart comes
to you my best thanks.

And you dare to add:
" in recognition of what I
owe you " as a compliment of
this dedication! Dio mio !!

You make me blush as I
blushed to day hearing the record
of puccinile made a few
years ago, pur troppo!
When shall I have the
pleasure to see you at River
side? I hope you may
be next week ... I want
very badly to ask you something
about your book —

With my best good wishes
very Cordially

Arturo Toscanini

To B. H. Haggin

cordial remembrance o'

(June 7th) Arturo Toscanini
1950

4

POSTSCRIPT—1979

The letter of resignation that NBC issued in facsimile had Toscanini addressing David Sarnoff as "My very dear David", and beginning with the statement that "seventeen years ago you sent me an invitation to become the Musical Director of an orchestra to be created especially for me." Since Toscanini knew the orchestra had not been created especially for him, the statement created doubts about the entire letter, exemplified by the questions of the NBC Symphony cellist Alan Shulman some years later, when he was giving me his recollections of Toscanini for *The Toscanini Musicians Knew: "Did* he resign? Did he do it of his own volition? Did *he* write that letter of resignation?" Shulman evidently was one of those who had not been convinced by Chotzinoff's account in 1956 of the circumstances leading to the letter, in the mélange of fact and fiction laced with malice that constituted the "intimate portrait" of Toscanini in his book. According to Chotzinoff, Toscanini had informed him, only a few days before the first rehearsal of *Un Ballo in Maschera*, that he no longer remembered the words of this opera and therefore requested him to cancel the project; but a day or two later he had informed Chotzinoff that he now remembered the words and could prepare and conduct the performance. This in fact he had done. But, said Chotzinoff, it had been clear to the Toscanini family that the time had come for him to stop; and Toscanini had agreed. At his request a letter of resignation had been prepared (presumably by Chotzinoff); and though weeks had passed without his signing it, during the week of the final broadcast he had "summoned the resolution to put his name to it and send it off."

But Guido Cantelli, who had seen Toscanini constantly during the season of 1953-54, when he had been in New York for engagements with the NBC Symphony and the New York Philharmonic, had reported to Jerome Toobin—manager of the former NBC Symphony when it continued on its own as the Symphony of the Air—what Toobin later told me: that in the fall of 1953 Walter Toscanini had informed his father, at Chotzinoff's request, of NBC's decision to discontinue the NBC Symphony broadcasts at the end of that season, and of Chotzinoff's suggestion that his father might, for appearances' sake, wish to resign; and that as a result there had been terrible scenes at Riverdale. It had been in the fall of 1953 that Walter Toscanini had written me about the decision at NBC to exclude everyone from his father's rehearsals, and that I had begun to hear of Toscanini's occasional confusion at the rehearsals, which had provided a possible reason for the exclusion. And so it had looked as if Toscanini's failing powers had led NBC to the decision Chotzinoff had communicated to Walter.

It was not until 1966, when I was recording Alfred Wallenstein's recollections for *The Toscanini Musicians Knew*, that I learned what Sarnoff had told him in private conversation in the fall of 1953: that Sarnoff and Chotzinoff had driven up to Riverdale to offer Toscanini a contract for the season of 1954-55, but had been intercepted in the driveway by Walter, who had requested them not to offer his father the contract, adding that he would not let him sign it. Presumably Walter had not told his father Sarnoff and Chotzinoff were coming; and not daring to tell him he had prevented them from offering him the contract, he had told him instead that NBC had decided to discontinue the broadcasts and suggested his resignation for appearances' sake. And presumably he had done this because of the family's belief that another season would be too much for Toscanini's diminishing physical strength.

But now we have the letter dated 16 May 1953, in Harvey Sachs's excellent new biography, in which Toscanini writes to a friend:

> I am not well, and no one believes me, the asses, but I'm not the same as I was. My eyes have worsened so much that I can no longer find glasses which can help me. My legs and

my memory fail me. I sleep little and badly, tormented by tragic, commonplace or fearful dreams. All in all, a poor unhappy man—and they have had the bad taste to force me to accept another year of concerts. And I, imbecile that I am, and tired of hearing myself bothered, have given in. The American public will again have to have the patience to put up with having an old man of 86 before its eyes.

It turns out, then, that when Walter Toscanini acted as he did in the fall of 1953 it was with the knowledge that his father himself realized he should reject the offer of another year of concerts but could not keep himself from accepting it. Walter may have felt that this justified his preventing Sarnoff from offering his father the additional year; but evidently foreseeing that his father might be angered by an intervention he considered presumptuous, Walter did not tell him what he had done. He must also have foreseen how his father would react to what he did tell him—i.e. that for Toscanini NBC's decision to end the broadcasts would be a decision to dismiss him, and as such an indignity without precedent, the shock of which would produce terrible scenes; but evidently Walter was not disquieted by the thought of the rage that would be directed not at him but at NBC. And he may not have foreseen what NBC musicians thought were in some degree consequences of this shock: the confusions at rehearsals, and the momentary breakdown at the final broadcast.

In addition to what Toscanini felt about the indignity to himself there was his grief and fury over the ruthless dismissal of his orchestra. David Walter, another member of that orchestra who gave me his recollections of Toscanini, related that whereas at the previous post-season parties for the orchestra in the '50s Toscanini had been "his old affable, congenial self", at the last such party in 1954 "he didn't come down to join us; and eventually Ghignatti and Cooley went upstairs to see him. They reported that he was in tears, exclaiming 'My poor orchestra! My poor orchestra!'—feeling that he was responsible for the disbanding of the orchestra, and that he couldn't face us." And Ghignatti, after a subsequent visit, reported Toscanini's referring to Sarnoff and Chotzinoff as *"animali"*.

One can understand, therefore, why the weeks passed without

Toscanini's being able to put an unusual shaky and blurred signature to the letter, prepared by one of the *"animali"*, that had him addressing the other one as "My very dear David" and beginning with the statement about "an orchestra to be created especially for me", which he knew to be untrue.

David Walter's words "his old affable, congenial self" described the Toscanini of the early NBC Symphony years, who, for example, on the sea voyage to South America in 1940 "walked the decks day and night, and was always approachable and affable and talked freely with the men." In those years, Walter said, "he was close to us"; whereas in later years "the entourage that made itself Toscanini's protector against the intrusion of the outside world included his orchestra among the intruders." And this at last provided an explanation of what until then I had been unable to account for—that after my encounter with Toscanini in June 1950 my letters brought no answers and I had no opportunity to talk with him again: apparently I too had been added to the intruders by the entourage—i.e. by Walter Toscanini, who lived in his father's house in Riverdale, where he was in a position to protect him against the intrusion not only of a business visit by David Sarnoff but of a personal letter that might lead to a visit by me.

Even now I don't think this action of Walter's in the period after 1950 represented ill-will; nor did that possibility occur to me at the time, since he continued to be cordial in personal encounters and correspondence: in the letter, for example, in which he informed me in November 1953 of the new rule at NBC that nobody was to be admitted to his father's rehearsals he expressed his regret, told me he had arranged that I receive tickets for the dress rehearsals, and closed with best wishes. However, sometime later in that season of 1953-54 Richard Gardner—an engineer at RCA Victor whom I had met when he was working on the transfer of Toscanini's broadcast *Otello* to commercial records, and whom I respected for his technical competence, ear for music, and conscientiousness—remarked with a grin one day that it might interest me to know Walter Toscanini had taken exception to my statements in *The Nation* about the Toscanini recordings. I *was* interested, but also was taken aback by this revelation not only of the fact of Walter's objection to what I had been writing, but of the fact that he had spoken of his objection to others, but not to me. I in turn said nothing about my discovery to him; but before I continue with what followed I must relate what had preceded—what had been happening to Toscanini's recordings that I had reported in *The Nation.*

Replying to Toscanini's letter of resignation in March 1954, Sarnoff wrote: "For the last seventeen years radio, television and the phonograph have done their best to transmit with the utmost fidelity your self-effacing, incomparable re-creations of the great music of the past and present . . . Happily, these instruments have recorded and preserved for us, and for posterity, the great music you have interpreted so faithfully and magnificently."

Actually—to begin with the broadcasts—what was transmitted by radio from Christmas night 1937 to April 1950 was the unnatural sound—unresonantly dry, flat, airlessly tight—that Toscanini's performances with the NBC Symphony had in NBC's acoustically dead Studio 8H filled with an audience. It was NBC's contention that this unnatural sound was what had to be broadcast for the listener to receive in his living room the normal spacious and lustrous sound of an orchestra in a resonant concert hall; but in fact the listener received in his living room the orchestra's unnaturally dry, flat, airlessly tight sound in Studio 8H; and he received the normal sound of an orchestra in a concert hall only on the infrequent occasions when the broadcast transmitted one of Toscanini's benefit concerts with the NBC Symphony in Carnegie Hall.

Though the sound in Studio 8H had inescapable defects, an engineer named Johnston found the one location for the microphone that produced the best in balance and clarity of the sound that could be achieved there. But in 1947 his successor, attempting to demonstrate that he could do better, used other microphone-placements that produced worse: sound that was shallower, less solid, and less clearly defined in the orchestral textures. And again in 1951, when NBC began to broadcast the performances from Carnegie Hall, it evidently did not adopt the microphone-placement CBS used for the New York Philharmonic, which produced the effect, for the radio listener, of placing the orchestra at a sufficient distance for him to hear its sound spaced out, balanced, and clear in texture; for the microphone-placement NBC's engineers did use produced the effect of bringing the orchestra too close to the radio listener for that spacing out, balance, and clarity of texture.

Moreover, comment on the broadcasts must include the fact that NBC, in the fall of 1947, moved Toscanini's broadcasts from Sunday at 5—a time when people were at leisure and could listen, and therefore a time which NBC could sell to Ford Motor Co. for another program—to Saturday at 6:30, which was not salable precisely because it was the time when people were busy with dinner and children and could not listen; the fact that whereas, in December 1947, NBC in New York added the required fifteen minutes from 6:15 to the 6:30 hour for Toscanini's broadcast of the first half of Verdi's *Otello*, its affiliated station in Rochester broadcast—in place of the first fifteen minutes of *Otello*—the regularly scheduled Answer Man program; and the fact that some of NBC's affiliated stations in major cities did not carry the Toscanini broadcasts live from New York, but scheduled at other inconvenient times recordings of the broadcasts on discs which, readers reported, occasionally were defective, or were played in incorrect order, or, as played, did not begin with the first grooves.

As for the Toscanini recordings, record companies always have claimed, like Sarnoff, that their recordings preserved the art of great performers for posterity, always without mentioning that this art would be preserved only as long as posterity bought the records in quantities which justified their continuing to be manufactured by the companies and kept in stock by the record stores. Actually, since the public buys mainly the recordings of the currently active performers whom it reads about in reviews of performances and publicity stories, the recordings of performers who no longer are active and written about are bought in decreasing quantities that eventually result in their being withdrawn from the catalogues. This happened even to the recordings of someone as famous as Toscanini; and an additional factor in his case was the advent of stereo, which made his mono recordings—even the ones with good mono sound—uninteresting to the large public that cared more about the latest in sound than about the greatest in performance.

It happened to some of the Toscanini recordings most important and treasurable for posterity—the ones he made with the New York Philharmonic in his final season with that orchestra in 1936, of their performances of Beethoven's Seventh, Brahms's Haydn Variations, Rossini's Overtures to *Semiramide* and *L'Italiana in Algeri*, and Wagner's Prelude to *Lohengrin*, his *Siegfried-Idyll*, and *Dawn and Siegfried's Rhine Journey* from *Die Götterdämmerung*. They are important because they preserve the phenomenal operation of the Philharmonic under Toscanini's direction, which he never duplicated with any other great orchestra; because they preserve this operation in performances which document his style of that early period—relaxed, expansive, articulating and organizing and shaping the substance of a work with much elasticity of tempo, and molding the phrase with much sharp inflection—as against the style of the later NBC Symphony years that was simpler, tauter, swifter, setting a tempo that was maintained with only slight modification, and giving the phrase only subtle inflection; and because they preserve these performances in sound of extraordinary fidelity and beauty. Equally important and treasurable for posterity—even with their less realistic and beautiful sound—are the recordings Toscanini made with the New York Philharmonic in 1929, of their performances of Haydn's Symphony No. 101 *(Clock)*, Mozart's Symphony K. 385 *(Haffner)*, the Scherzo from Mendelssohn's music for *A Midsummer Night's Dream*, Rossini's Overture to *The Barber of Seville*, and the Preludes to Acts 1 and 3 of Verdi's *La Traviata*. But at this moment I find only the 1929 Prelude to Act 1 of *La Traviata* and the 1936 Beethoven Seventh still listed as available for posterity in the Schwann catalogue of mono recordings.

Additional documentation of Toscanini's more effective and impressive earlier style is provided by his first recordings, in 1938 and 39, with the NBC Symphony, of Haydn's Symphony No. 88, Mozart's Symphony in G minor, Beethoven's Symphonies Nos. 3 *(Eroica)*, 5 and 8, the Lento and Vivace from Beethoven's Quartet Op. 135, Rossini's Overture to *William Tell*, and Paganini's *Moto Perpetuo*. These document also the extraordinary energy and fire of the performances of those first years, in which Toscanini was stimulated by the exceptional capacities and responsiveness of the many young string virtuosos in the orchestra, and they were stimulated by his awesome powers, magnetism and dedication. And of these performances too I find only those of the two movements of Beethoven's Quartet Op. 135 and Paganini's *Moto Perpetuo* listed in the Schwann catalogue.[1]

As for the many recordings Toscanini made with the NBC Symphony in the last ten years of his career—with few exceptions the only ones available on RCA records in recent years—most of them are still listed in the Schwann catalogue; but already deleted are those of Haydn's Symphonies Nos. 98 and 99, Mozart's Symphonies K.385 *(Haffner)*, 543, 550 (in G minor) and 551 *(Jupiter)* and his Divertimento K.287, Beethoven's *Missa Solemnis*, Schubert's Symphony No. 9 (the 1953 recording), Mendelssohn's *Italian* Symphony, Berlioz's *Harold in Italy* and *Romeo and Juliet*, Act 2 of Gluck's *Orfeo ed Euridice*, Verdi's *Un Ballo in Maschera, Otello* and Act 4 of *Rigoletto*, Strauss's *Death and Transfiguration* and *Don Quixote*, and Prokofiev's *Classical Symphony*. And presumably the deletions will continue.

So much for Sarnoff's claim that the RCA recordings would preserve Toscanini's performances for posterity. And disputable also, in the second place, was his claim of their "utmost fidelity"—as disputable when made for the recordings as when made for the broadcasts. Actually, the sound of many of the NBC Symphony recordings was in varying degree defective; and the recordings with defective sound, contrary to general belief, were not all made in acoustically deficient Studio 8H: some were made in acoustically excellent Carnegie Hall; and on the other hand some with excellent sound were made in 8H. The fact is that when the sound of a recording, whether made in 8H or in Carnegie Hall, was defective, the reason was not the acoustical

[1] The performances in that early style that Toscanini recorded between 1937 and 1939 with the BBC Symphony in London will be dealt with on pp. 144-5, and the ones he recorded with the Philadelphia Orchestra in 1941-42 on pp. 135-9, 145.

deficiencies of 8H anymore, obviously, than it was the acoustical excellence of Carnegie Hall, but was the deficiencies in technical competence and personal intelligence and character of the men who supervised the making of the recordings—the producers who told the engineers where to place the microphones and what to do with their tone-controls, all of which affected the sound imprinted on wax or acetate or, later, tape. The superb-sounding Debussy *Ibéria* Toscanini recorded at his last session in 8H on 2 June 1950 demonstrated that first-rate recordings could be made there when the producer—in this case Richard Mohr—had the single microphone placed at what Johnston had found to be its optimum location in 8H, and—as Johnston also had found to be necessary—had the rows of seats pushed all the way toward the back wall to increase the studio's resonance. And the consequences of not doing what Johnston recommended were demonstrated by the lessened presence and distinctness of the beautiful sound of the Debussy *La Mer* for which, the day before, Mohr chose to have the microphone placed a few feet back from the Johnston location, and the rows of seats pushed only part of the way back. Even more striking was the demonstration provided by two recordings made at the session in 8H on 18 May 1945: the Gershwin *An American in Paris* with spacious, clear and warm sound, which the producer, Richard Gilbert, achieved by following Johnston's recommendations; and the Sousa *Stars and Stripes Forever* with coarse sound lacking spaciousness and depth, which Gilbert produced by placing microphones, in accordance with an idea of his own, everywhere except the Johnston location. As for Carnegie Hall, the location of the single microphone with which NBC obtained the beautiful and perfectly balanced sound of the broadcast performances of Verdi's *Requiem* and Beethoven's *Missa Solemnis* in 1940 was known; but Gilbert in 1947 took it into his head to place the microphone further back, and in addition to cover the side boxes and parquet with draperies, producing in this way the lusterless, compressed sound of the Tchaikovsky *Pathétique*; and he produced the even dimmer, weaker sound of the Mendelssohn *Midsummer Night's Dream* music by placing the microphone—for this lightly scored music!—even further back and higher. And Mohr, recording the

Missa Solemnis in 1953, rejected what was done in 1940, and produced with his own placing of microphones the sound in which the chorus predominated over soloists and orchestra.

Thus, whereas it would have been unthinkable that anyone should change what Toscanini produced at a concert, an RCA producer could, and did, change it when Toscanini produced it for a recording, and achieved with his changes, in many cases, a defective transformation instead of the facsimile that correct microphone-placement and manipulation of tone-controls would have achieved. Moreover, the advent of tape gave producers and editors an additional means of changing what Toscanini had produced. Before the days of tape, what was imprinted on wax or acetate could not be altered when it was transferred to the metal master, from the master to the stamper, and from the stamper to the final disc; but the sound imprinted on tape, after being heard and approved by Toscanini, could be, and was, altered—for example, by stepping up or cutting down treble or bass—when it was transferred to the working tape used in the processing of the metal parts for the production of the final discs. Thus the superb sound imprinted on the original tape of Musorgsky's *Pictures at an Exhibition* was altered in the transfer to RCA Victor LM-1838 by an extreme treble boost that produced the ear-piercing solo trumpet at the beginning, the snarling brass in *Catacombs*, the harsh violins and raucous tuttis. Tape made it possible also to modify the sound of an already issued recording: one made a new transfer from the original tape to a new working tape incorporating the desired modifications. This was done with the Debussy *La Mer* already issued on LM-1221: new records for LM-1221 replaced the excellent first transfer with a new transfer—made by the RCA technician Gerhardt whom Walter Toscanini had engaged in 1950 to transfer the acetate recordings of Toscanini's broadcasts to tape—in which the original sound was "enhanced" (RCA's term) by artificial echo-chamber resonance that put a false electronic gloss on the sounds of violins, violas, cellos and woodwinds, softened and diffused the solid and cleanly defined chords, drum beats and bass notes into an indeterminate heavy rumble, and produced a liquefying and blurring of the over-all sound. And still not satisfied, Gerhardt later made for LM-1833 yet another transfer that inflicted even more "enhancement" on the sound with more damaging effect.[2]

Gerhardt, in the early '50s, continued his "enhancement" of new and old recordings, spoiling good sound and making poor sound worse. It might have seemed reasonable to try to improve the unresonantly dry, compressed and otherwise poor sound of the 1949 Beethoven *Eroica* issued on LM-1042; but this turned out to be more real and acceptable than the electronic gloss and liquefaction and blur of the first "enhanced" version in LM-6900 (the 1953 de luxe limited edition of the nine symphonies), and of the second one substituted for the original in LM-1042. On the other hand the bright, clear and solid sound of the original 78-rpm recording of Mozart's Divertimento K. 287, transferred without change to LP on LM-13, needed no improvement; and what the "enhancement" and treble and bass boosts of the later transfer to LM-2001 did was to make the violins too bright and glossy and rob the too heavy basses of definition and solidity.[3]

There was, from the beginning, the question of what Toscanini thought about all these matters. Since he did not, in our conversations, ever refer to what I wrote in *The Nation* about the sound in Studio 8H, live or on records, I did not question him about it, and accepted what the men in the orchestra told me: that whereas they hated 8H because they couldn't hear each other in it, he liked it because, standing on the podium, he could

[2] The falsified Musorgsky *Pictures* was declared by the reviewers to be the high-water mark of RCA recording of Toscanini; and Roland Gelatt wrote in *High Fidelity* that the "enhancement" gave the *La Mer* on LM-1833 "the atmosphere of a concert hall", which was "a real improvement", adding only that electronic trickery could not give it "the clarity, brilliance and presence" of the Musorgsky *Pictures*. Marsh too heard in the *La Mer* on LM-1833 "the effect of a hall recording . . . offering more brilliance, solidity, and a wider dynamic range."

[3] For reasons that will appear later I mention that with these altered versions being substituted for the originals, sometimes under the old record numbers, I thought it advisable to provide the discography in the 1959 edition of this book with the stamper numbers of the successive versions—i.e. the numbers like 5s or 20s immediately following serial numbers like E2RP 1325 on the blank portion of the record surface—by which old and new versions could be identified. And I also provided the settings of equalization- and tone-controls that I recommended for them.

hear everything clearly. I accepted this because I knew that what he demanded in performance, live or recorded, was that it enable him to hear everything he had read in the score. And so, listening the first time to the marvelous-sounding recording of Debussy's *Ibéria*, I was startled by the suddenly altered sound at No. 48 in the second movement—its lessened brightness, the lessened brilliance of the violins' climactic phrase, and the amazing fact that the sustained F-sharp of the basses couldn't be heard at all. When I inquired about this Mohr and Walter Toscanini acted as if it were news to them; but then I encountered statements by Gelatt and Marsh—seemingly based on information from RCA Victor—that Toscanini had approved release of the 1950 recording only after the passage in the second movement had been replaced by a splice-in of the passage from an earlier broadcast performance. (Gelatt found the spliced-in passage "undetectable to my ear", and Marsh said it "cannot be heard".) And in 1958 Mohr read to me a letter in which Walter, in 1952, had informed Victor of his father's request of the spliced-in passage. I thought I knew the reason for Toscanini's insistence on the splice-in: the heightened plasticity and grace of the melodic phrasing; nevertheless I was astounded by the inconsistency of his refusal to accept the sound of the timpani in Tchaikovsky's *Romeo and Juliet* that had been clearly audible but not as strong as he thought it should be, and his acceptance of the completely inaudible F-sharp of the basses in the *Ibéria*.

As for the falsification of the sound of his recordings by "enhancement" in the early '50s, I was no longer in contact with Toscanini in this period and therefore had no opportunity to learn what he thought of the "enhanced" versions or even whether he heard them. I knew that he heard the original tape of a recording, since Victor had to have his approval of a recording before issuing it; but I did not know whether Victor had to have his approval also of the edited working tape made for the processing of the records, and of each new working tape for a later release, and whether, therefore, he had heard these working tapes. I was inclined to think they did *not* require his approval and he therefore had *not* heard them; since I found it difficult to believe he would have approved the monstrously falsified *La Mer* on LM-1833 if he had heard it. But this was mere specula-

tion; whereas Gerhardt asserted as fact—to someone who reported his statement to me—that Toscanini *had* approved the
"enhanced" *La Mer.* And this was the basis of my statement on
page 88 that Gerhardt "seems to have been able to persuade
Toscanini to substitute his in some instances monstrously falsified 'enhanced' versions for the originals"—which in time I discovered was not true.

To return now to what Gardner reported early in 1954: since
in the many years that I had written in *The Nation* about
Toscanini's work with the NBC Symphony there had been no
objection by Walter Toscanini to my comments on the defective sound of the broadcasts and many of the recordings, I was
unprepared for his objection to what I had written in the fall of
1953: the letter in which I had expressed to him my concern over
the "defects that could not possibly have been in the test records
that your father heard . . . and that were sometimes the result of
monkeying with the recording . . . after your father had heard it
and approved of what he heard"—this in the belief that he
shared my concern and would agree that "surely your father's
work should not be tampered with and falsified in this way; and
surely there must be some way of . . . keeping the recordings
under his control;" and my *Nation* article on the same subject,
which I had assumed he would welcome because of its possible
effect on Victor. But, as I said earlier, since he hadn't expressed
his objection to me, I didn't question him about it; and it was
explained in the course of time and events.

In the summer of 1955 Gardner was assigned to work with
Toscanini—in the laboratory Walter Toscanini had created in
the basement of his father's house—on recordings that were to be
derived from the NBC Symphony broadcasts. (Though Gardner
told me he was to work only on these new recordings, he also
produced the better-sounding new versions of Beethoven's nine
symphonies in newly numbered LM-6901 and on the old-num-
bered single records, but presumably not the other new versions
of previously issued recordings that continued to appear.) And in
an article about this work in *High Fidelity* Gardner recounted
Toscanini's having explained how the introduction of artificial
echo-chamber resonance damaged recorded sound. This revealed

for the first time Toscanini's dislike of that form of "enhancement"; and in conversation on later occasions Gardner told me of other incidents in which Toscanini had exhibited this dislike: his having rejected, because of its "enhanced" sound, the first version of the recording of Verdi's *Requiem* derived from the 1951 broadcast; his having compelled Victor to withdraw the already issued recording of Strauss's *Death and Transfiguration* after he had listened to a copy he was planning to take to Geraldine Farrar and heard with outrage what had been done to the sound he had approved. From this I learned that Toscanini, after approving the original tape of a recording, normally did not listen to the subsequent working tape; and I felt certain that he hadn't even heard the "enhanced" *La Mer*, much less approved it as Gerhardt claimed.

In addition there was what I learned in 1955 from Victor's Administrator of Recording, A. A. Pulley. The copy of a letter to him, in which I asked about the changes in the recording of Musorgsky's *Pictures*, has my notations of what he told me on the telephone: that after being informed by Walter Toscanini that his father had not approved the original tape of Musorgsky's *Pictures*, Pulley had received a letter in which Walter wrote that his father had found the sound to be "logy and heavy" and had requested that echo-chamber resonance be added and whatever else be done that would brighten it; and that subsequently the edited tape representing what Pulley referred to as "conferences with Gerhardt" had been approved by Toscanini. And this, it turned out, was one instance of what Pulley described as standard practice. Since Victor dealt with Toscanini through Walter, what happened was that Gerhardt told Walter what he wanted to do with the sound of a recording, which Walter then communicated to Victor as what his father wanted done, and which Victor then told Gerhardt to do. This left me certain, now, that Toscanini not only had not heard and approved the falsified Musorgsky *Pictures* which Victor was told he had approved, but *had* approved the superb original *Pictures* that Victor was told he had not approved.

Thus I discovered that it was not Toscanini but Walter whom Gerhardt had persuaded to substitute his "enhanced" versions of the recordings for the originals. And I thought I understood not only why he had been able to persuade Walter to do this, but why Walter had objected to my unfavorable comments on the substituted versions. As someone musically ungifted Walter did not benefit from being the son of a musical genius; and as the son of an enemy to Mussolini he lost his rare-book business in Milan and had to come here to make a new start. Since he had been interested in the recording process, and had even attempted to record his father's performances, he made this new start with RCA Victor—initially to learn the record business, but, as it turned out, to assist the company and his father in their dealings with each other. And very early, with his interest in the recording process, he was able to do one thing for them which gave him a feeling of personal achievement. That is, perceiving that his father rejected recordings which, when played back to him on the poor reproducing equipment of the '30s and '40s, did not produce what he had heard in the performance he had conducted, Walter got a Victor research engineer named Snepvangers (who later worked on the long-playing record introduced by Columbia) to assemble components of a sound system which created in Toscanini's living room an approximation, in quality and volume, of the sound he was accustomed to hearing about him as he conducted an orchestra—with the result that he was satisfied by recordings he might otherwise have rejected, and approved them for release. On the other hand, with the interest in the recording process that caused Walter to be impressed, ten years later, by Gerhardt's ideas for electronically "enhancing" the sound of his father's recordings, but without the musical gift that would have enabled him to recognize the damage this "enhancement" inflicted on them, he used his position to have Gerhardt's versions issued in place of his father's originals. And this time Walter's own feeling of personal achievement was increased by the all but unanimous approval of the record-reviewers—after which he could not read with anything but shock and anger my dissenting report on what he had achieved.

It was not until March 1956 that—in a letter in which I expressed to Walter my happiness that Gardner was working with his father and my eagerness to know what they had produced—I mentioned having been told once that he had taken exception to my statements about his father's recordings and asked him to tell me what he had objected to. In his reply, which ended as always with his best wishes, he wrote that he could not remember any details of his having taken exception to my comments on the recordings, and added that with all the confusion about so-called high fidelity, the more he worked in this field the more he believed that everyone was entitled to his own opinion.

What Walter couldn't remember in this exchange he did remember in a later one. Of the recordings produced by Toscanini and Gardner from broadcasts the Berlioz *Harold in Italy* was issued by Victor in the summer of 1956 and the Strauss *Don Quixote* in the fall; but months and years passed without the release of one especially important and impatiently awaited recording that Toscanini was known to have approved before his death in 1957—the one of the Berlioz *Romeo and Juliet* he had broadcast in 1947. The reason was that Munch—who was still conducting the Boston Symphony and recording for Victor—had made a recording of Berlioz's *Romeo* which Victor wanted to protect from the competition of Toscanini's recording. In 1960, when Toscanini's 1953 Beethoven *Eroica* was issued, the word from Victor was that it was about to release his *Romeo*, which nevertheless it did not do. And the next word from Victor, early in 1962, was that it would release the Toscanini *Romeo* if it could obtain good enough source material of the 1947 broadcast (but the true reason for the further delay was revealed in the fall of 1962, when Victor issued Munch's remake of his *Romeo* in stereo: this new Munch recording now had to be protected from the competition of the Toscanini recording).

I wrote to Walter Toscanini, in February 1962, that I couldn't understand Victor's making this statement about the need of good enough source material, which—in the light of his father's approval of the completed recording—made no sense. And in his reply—concerned not with what was in my letter but with what was on his mind—he said he did not understand why Victor's decision not to release any more Toscanini recordings made no sense to me. He went on to explain to me what I knew: that the record companies were businesses that had to make money by producing what would be bought; and what was being bought was the new recordings of Reiner and Munch in the new stereo sound, not the old recordings of Toscanini in mono sound. And for this he blamed what he called the entire tribe of reviewers from Irving Kolodin to myself, all of whom were concerned with the sound of the recordings instead of with the musical performances, and none of whom had ever found the sound of even one of his father's recordings good enough. Could Victor be blamed for its decision, he continued, when I had found fault with all the Toscanini recordings it had issued—when I had filled every page in the discography of *Conversations with Toscanini* with the defects in the sound, and had made readers think they could get decent reproduction of the recordings only by manipulation of the controls available on expensive equipment? (I had sent him a copy of *Conversations* in 1959; and his first and only direct comment to me on the book was this denunciation of the discography.)

I sent Walter two pages of typescript filled with quotations—from my reviews in *The Nation* and *The New Republic,* and from the text and discography of *Conversations with Toscanini*—some of which reported the excellent sound of the recording, and others, after reporting imperfect or poor sound, urged acquisition of the great performance that was imperfectly reproduced in preference to the beautiful-sounding performance that was musically less effective. And in my long accompanying letter I said, among other things, that he failed to recognize the difference—which others did recognize—between this writing of mine and the writing of the others in the "tribe of reviewers" who were most concerned with the mono sound of the Toscanini recordings and its occasional defects, not with the unique musical quality of the performances. Thanking me for this material, Walter added that he hadn't wanted me to go through all that labor and trouble.

This was in a letter, in April 1962, in which he also inquired whether I had heard the WQXR broadcast of the unreleased Philadelphia Orchestra recordings of 1941-42, on which he said work was still being done in Riverdale to reduce their surface noises. And before I continue I should amplify and correct my statement in parentheses on page 23, which represents my knowledge and understanding at the time I wrote it, but not what I learned subsequently. Whereas on the one hand, the statements about the *Death and Transfiguration, La Mer* and *Queen Mab*

on pages 24 and 25 represent my own first-hand experience—i.e.
what I heard when I listened to the test pressings with Toscanini
in 1942, and what he said on that occasion—on the other hand,
the statement in parentheses on page 23 about the noisy defects
and low volume-level represents what Walter Toscanini *reported*
to me later as the findings of Victor's Quality Control Department concerning recordings I took to be the ones I had not
heard—of Schubert's Ninth, Mendelssohn's *Midsummer Night's
Dream* music, Tchaikovsky's *Pathétique* and Debussy's *Ibéria*.
Whether they were also the findings of his father concerning
these recordings Walter did not say, and I do not know; but I do
know they were not his findings concerning the ones I listened to
with him. These all began very softly, which would have made
any noisy defect obtrusive and disturbing; but no such noise
disturbed him; and the reason for his rejection of the third side
of the *La Mer* was not noises but an imbalance in the recorded
musical sound of the performance that prevented his hearing
one of the woodwinds.

Both the sides found to be musically defective by Toscanini
and the ones found to be technically defective by Victor's
Quality Control Department were to be re-recorded; but the
union ban on recording delayed the re-recording for two years.
Though the Philadelphia Orchestra, by the time the ban ended,
had transferred from Victor to Columbia, it was available for the
re-recording of the rejected sides of its recordings with Toscanini.
But when nothing happened, and I inquired, Walter Toscanini
told me that Victor wanted to abandon the Philadelphia Orchestra recordings and have his father make new ones with the
NBC Symphony (for Victor there was no difference between a
Toscanini performance with the Philadelphia and a Toscanini
performance with the NBC Symphony), and that "we are trying
to get father to forget the Philadelphia recordings"—which I understood to mean that the decision was Victor's, and the task of
persuading Toscanini was Walter's. He didn't tell me why Victor wanted to abandon the Philadelphia recordings; and I could
only conjecture (erroneously, as I learned only recently) that it
didn't want Toscanini's name to promote what was now a Columbia orchestra, and was willing to sacrifice the recordings to
prevent it. The argument that the Philadelphia Orchestra was

now a Columbia orchestra would not have counted for much with Toscanini; and Walter could hardly argue that the performances were poor; but he could, and did successfully, argue that the recordings were mechanically defective beyond hope of remedy. This must have happened before 1950; for I remember Toscanini commenting bitterly about it, "I worked like a dog!" And I heard nothing more about the recordings until Walter's mention of them in April 1962.

Presumably I expressed my surprise; for in a letter in June 1962 he said yes, he was issuing the Philadelphia recordings in spite of his father's inability to make up his mind about them, because their flaws were too insignificant for the entire performances to be sacrificed. Victor was considering issuing the Schubert Ninth in the fall; and he would be grateful if I would come up and listen to it and perhaps give Victor a push in the right direction in one of my articles. In January 1963 he confirmed that Station WRVR in New York was going to broadcast the entire series of his father's NBC broadcasts from tapes prepared in Riverdale by John Corbett, the highly competent engineer who had been working there for several years. And a couple of months later WRVR broadcast Corbett's tape of the Schubert Ninth that Victor was to issue in the fall.[4]

The broadcast was introduced by Marsh's account of the history of the Philadelphia recordings and what had made it possible now to issue the Schubert Ninth—an account which turned out later to have been his lurid "enhancement" of the Victor statement in the brochure accompanying the record issued in the fall of 1963: namely that the recording hadn't been issued twenty years earlier because of the "mechanical imperfections which neither the Maestro nor the company could accept," but could be issued now because of the "[restoration of] the recording to its original state" by Corbett's "750 hours of work". "I heard this material some years ago," said Marsh, "from the Victor acetate records which were sent to Toscanini. They were really pretty horrible: the noise level was as high as the levels of

[4] For reasons that will appear I mention here a reference, in a letter from Walter in September 1962, to the copy of a private recording— made in Riverdale "For Walter Toscanini and His Friends"—that he said he had allotted to me as a friend.

the music in the pianissimo passages." But the new tape Corbett had processed from the original metal parts "[conveyed] all the familiar warm round sound of the Philadelphia Orchestra" that Marsh had been unable to hear through the noise of the test records sent to Toscanini.

I told the musical director of WRVR, a Mr. De Witt, that Marsh's statements were contradicted by what Toscanini and I had heard when we listened to the test records in 1942, as I could demonstrate with the test records of the Schubert Ninth that I now had. De Witt offered to record my corrective statement for a few minutes of the next broadcast; and I did record a brief statement and a few passages from the test records to demonstrate that even in pianissimo passages the surface noise was not disturbingly obtrusive, did not prevent one's hearing the beautiful sound, and therefore did not justify Victor's having withheld the recordings twenty years earlier. The "mechanical imperfections" had been exaggerated, I said, in order to provide that justification for an action whose real reason, I thought, was Victor's desire to keep Toscanini's name from benefitting a Columbia orchestra.

De Witt asked me if I intended to inform Walter Toscanini of my reply to Marsh; and I assured him of my intention to do so. But my letter did not reach Walter until after De Witt had shown him my reply to Marsh and had acceded to his request that it not be broadcast, and until after Walter had written me a letter which, as it happened, arrived together with his reply to mine. A friend who read the two letters looked up at one point to remark, "Walter Toscanini didn't inherit anything else from his father; but he did inherit his temper;" and when he had finished reading he said: "This is a man who in all these years has achieved no understanding of your service to his father . . . a man in whom in all these years you have created no good will and trust; and he is a [obscenity] whom you should have nothing more to do with." My reply to Walter was to quote this statement and say I would do what my friend advised.

A few years ago I happened to mention to someone who had been with RCA Victor a number of years my conjecture that Victor had withheld the Philadelphia recordings in order to keep Toscanini's name from benefitting a Columbia orchestra. "I think you are mistaken about that," he said. "What you must remember is that Victor had a lot of money invested in those recordings and didn't want to lose it. And from what I've been told it was Walter Toscanini who made all the fuss about the defects of the recordings and persuaded his father to reject them. Victor had to accept that; and when Walter decided to release the Schubert Ninth, Victor had to offer an explanation for issuing now what it had withheld twenty years earlier." Thus I discovered that Walter, not Victor, had been the prime mover in the affair, and began to understand why he had been enraged by my demonstration that the official explanation of the withholding and issuing of the recording was not true.

Though I had no further contacts with Walter Toscanini, I had what might be described as indirect experiences with him, which were as revealing as my earlier direct ones. But his operation in them is best illustrated by an example which did not involve me. Marsh has recently stressed the fact that in the writing of his book he had access to "the family archive assembled by ... Walter Toscanini"; and in the preface to the 1962 second edition he wrote that Walter had "gone over the text [of the 1956 first edition] with me, pointing out mistakes and setting them right"—a procedure which again had "taken us to the Toscanini family papers." But the examining of documents in this and other archives did not prevent Marsh from writing in 1956—about Toscanini's operation at the working rehearsals Marsh had never observed, and in the performances he had been unable to hear and evaluate correctly—statements like those about the recorded performances of the *Tristan* excerpts on pp. 98-99, which one NBC Symphony musician characterized as "nonsense" and "pure stupidity"; and equally worthless statements about the personal character and behavior of the man with whom he had never exchanged a word. And not only the reappearance of these statements in the 1962 edition, but the nature of the three changes I discovered that could be attributed to Walter Toscanini—one concerned with his father, the other two with Cantelli and myself—indicated that when going over the text with Marsh (apparently less exhaustively than Marsh claimed) he had his mind on other matters than correction of error about his father.

To begin with the change that did concern his father: Marsh repeated in 1962 his assertion that "Toscanini brooks no peers" and "his comments on his rivals ... lacked charity," although Walter undoubtedly had, like me, heard his father speak well of Nikisch, and seen his face light up as he recalled Schuch; and on the other hand had, like me, heard his father's descriptions of the specific musical defects he perceived in the performances of Muck, Beecham, Stokowski, Koussevitzky and the rest. What Walter did get Marsh to change in 1962 was the further assertion that "young conductors were able ... to make friends with the Maestro and enjoy a pleasant relationship with him until they became potential rivals, after which the friendship abruptly ceased"—Marsh's examples being Rodzinski and Steinberg, whom one cannot conceive of Toscanini regarding as potential rivals. And the change was merely the omission of the last eleven words and substitution of "so long as he was permitted a dominant role"—which was not true in the case of the only such young conductor known to me, Cantelli.

So we come to the more consequential change Walter got Marsh to make in his paragraph on Cantelli. In the first edition, after mentioning Toscanini's praise of Cantelli and quoting his statement that Cantelli was "the only one who plays music as I do," Marsh took the usual line with Cantelli—that of the experienced critic who could discern the as yet unfulfilled promise of a young conductor, whose gift, he contended, was "essentially lyrical", and who "in attempting to combine with his melodic sensitivity the overpowering motor energy of Toscanini ... seemed to be making an effort to play works on a larger scale than his understanding of them permitted without pretension and distortion," and had yet to "develop an approach of his own that is more in keeping with his powers." ("Nonsensical," said the NBC musician. "The opposite is true: though he matured, his large-scale motor energy was there from the start—in his Musorgsky *Pictures at an Exhibition,* for example, which was tremendous. His style didn't change: he got to know things better.") But in the revised 1962 edition I noted the insertion, after Toscanini's praise of Cantelli, of the statement "though Toscanini seems to have been more impressed by Cantelli's artistic dedication than his musicianship *per se;*" and it took time to discover where Marsh had picked up this idea that was contradicted by a number of facts. First and most important was the fact that Toscanini had invited, and continued to invite, Cantelli to conduct his NBC Symphony, which he would do only to someone with outstanding musical gifts. Moreover, recommending Cantelli to the Philadelphia Orchestra for a pair of concerts which Munch couldn't conduct because of illness, Toscanini wrote: "... I can assure you that the Philadelphia public will find in young Cantelli a musically sound and exciting conductor, and you will be as proud as I was when I introduced him with my orchestra in four extremely successful concerts." At Cantelli's rehearsals in Studio 8H I had seen Toscanini nodding his approval and smiling his pleasure; and years later the NBC Symphony cellist Alan Shulman recalled Toscanini, at those rehearsals, "beaming like a proud father. If he had had a son who was musically gifted, this was what he would have wanted him to be." However it turned out that Toscanini's actual musically ungifted son also had observed this at the rehearsals, and that his resentment had led him to make, in a broadcast after Cantelli's and Toscanini's deaths, the false assertion that he got Marsh to insert in his book, about Toscanini's having been impressed more by Cantelli's dedication than by his musical gifts.

So with Marsh's report on the recording of Debussy's *Ibéria:* Walter did not question Marsh's questionable surmise that Toscanini's reason for not conducting *Gigues* and *Rondes de Printemps,* the other two works of *Images,* may have been his inability to understand them; but he did get Marsh to add, in the 1962 edition, that "the insertion of a few bars of broadcast material into the second movement has produced a greater eruption of extravagant nonsense than anything ever done to a Toscanini recording. . . . It was done on Toscanini's insistence, so the critic who protests sets himself up to protect Toscanini's art from Toscanini, a posture of arrogance which the Maestro found intolerable." The writing can give the impression that it was Toscanini himself who expressed his annoyance in conversation with Marsh; but as far as I know he never met Toscanini; and I recognize Walter's thinking in the misinterpretation of my report of the insertion of the broadcast passage as a protest and an intolerably presumptuous attempt to protect Toscanini's work from Toscanini.

I hear Walter Toscanini's voice also in the following passage from the letter of Thomas E. Patronite of Cleveland, an officer of the Beecham Society, in the June 1967 issue of the magazine *High Fidelity* about my review of the Victor album *A Toscanini Treasury of Historic Broadcasts:* "This gentleman parlayed a few pleasantries with the Maestro into his book *Conversations with Toscanini* and proceeded to set forth what must be the most monumental example of nit-picking of all time: in his evaluation of the Toscanini discs then on the market, he went so far as to list the preferred matrix numbers." While it is possible that Patronite got this description of my book from Walter himself, I think it more probable that he got it through Marsh when he was in Cleveland gathering material for his book about the Cleveland Orchestra.

But others did get Walter's statements directly from him. In 1967, when the University of Texas was negotiating with him about material for its library, he expressed to one of its representatives his unhappiness about the book of interviews I had just published, *The Toscanini Musicians Knew,* which he said claimed a close relation to his father that I had not had. This in the face of my explicit statement on p. 66 of *Conversations*—that "my meetings with Toscanini were few and infrequent and limited in scope; and I didn't get to know him as his intimates did . . ."

Walter also was visited by Clyde Key of the Toscanini Society, who later—angered by my criticism of his selection of Toscanini performances for distribution to the society's members—included in a bulletin to those members, in August 1973, an account of our disagreements in which he wrote: "We have been told by a source in a position to know that this critic's invitation to Maestro's rehearsals in Carnegie Hall near the end of Maestro's career were withdrawn because of his interference in matters which did not concern him"—presumably at the rehearsals. Since I had done nothing there but observe and listen, it occurred to me to look up the letter in which Walter had informed me with regret of NBC's new rule excluding everyone from the rehearsals; and finding it was dated 23 November 1953, I looked up my *Nation* article of that week, and found that I had described and denounced in that article the damaging of Toscanini's recordings with "enhancement"—a matter that did concern the critic who reviewed recordings for readers of *The Nation*. Thus I discovered at last that it had been Walter who had excluded me from the rehearsals because of what I had written about the recordings.

And only a few months ago a Chicago reader sent me Marsh's review in the Chicago *Sun-Times* of the new Harvey Sachs biography of Toscanini, in which Marsh wrote that "Toscanini broke with Haggin for good reasons. As Walter Toscanini explained to me many years ago, Toscanini was offended by Haggin's inflexible opinions and his presumption to question the maestro's musical judgment. Moreover, he was distrustful of Haggin's implication that he, rather than Toscanini, should be evaluating the technical quality of the Toscanini records and determining the music the great man should perform and record. Apparently a decisive exchange was over the music of Brahms, which Toscanini adored and Haggin considered pretentious." This, clearly, was Walter's version of my last encounter with Toscanini on 1 June 1950, which I describe on pp. 87-90, and which not only was different from what Walter said, but did not have the result he said it had—to judge from the fact that after our smiling exchanges that afternoon Toscanini inscribed to me the photograph I had brought to him, I attended his two recording sessions, he recorded *Ibéria* as I had urged, I continued to attend his rehearsals until November 1953, and he sent me his Christmas card in 1955.

5

THE TOSCANINI RECORDINGS—1979

First the great early performances with the New York Philharmonic, BBC Symphony and Philadelphia Orchestras.

Of the 1936 New York Philharmonic performances transferred to LP only the one of Beethoven's Symphony No. 7 is available on American RCA Victrola VIC-1502, whose sound, when I heard it years ago, fluctuated in volume and brightness and had less than its original solidity (increase bass). It is also on German RCA AT-153, which I haven't heard.[1] The 1929 Philharmonic Haydn Symphony No. 101 (Clock) is available only on AT-130, coupled with the superb 1938 NBC Symphony performance of Haydn's No. 88, in sound that is reported to me to be poor and afflicted with echo-chamber resonance. And the 1929 Prelude to Verdi's La Traviata is included on RCA CRM1-2494, with NBC Symphony performances of Beethoven's Fifth, the Overture to Rossini's The Barber of Seville and Waldteufel's Skaters Waltz, all in good sound.

Of the BBC Symphony performances the ones of Beethoven's Symphonies Nos. 1 and 4 are available in good sound on English World Record Club SH-134, and No. 6 (Pastoral) on SH-112. Seraphim 60150 has Mozart's Overture to The Magic Flute, Rossini's to La Scala di Seta and Beethoven's Leonore No. 1, all in good sound (but increase treble in all three, and reduce bass in

[1] All references to AT numbers (except to the English AT-111 under Debussy), are those of German RCA's Toscanini Edition which are imported by Bremen House Inc., 218 East 86 Street, New York, N. Y. 10028, and are available in other record stores. I don't receive them for review.

the last two), with the Weber-Berlioz *Invitation to the Dance* in poor sound. Avoid the poor-sounding earlier versions of all these pieces on Seraphim 6015.

In 1976, thirteen years after the release of the Philadelphia Orchestra Schubert Ninth, all the 1941-42 performances with this orchestra were issued at last on RCA CRM5-1900. In the accompanying notes it was David Hall this time who related the story not only of the disturbing noises but of the damaged sound that he reported having heard in 1942; [2] but the occasional clicks and other noises that one hears now represent the deteriorated state of the metal masters; and the sound derived from those deteriorated masters hasn't the amplitude, depth and solidity of the sound from the test pressings of 1942. One would have heard little noise and beautiful sound if the original recordings had been issued in the '40s; but even the ones issued in 1976, with bass and treble increased, produce what one can hear is marvelous playing by the orchestra under Toscanini, and his marvelous shaping of the music in his expansive style of that period, which makes most of the performances more effective than the later ones with the NBC Symphony. This must be added about the Schubert Ninth: the version issued in 1963 on RCA LD-2663 had more amplitude and solidity than the one issued in CRM5-1900, which appears to have been newly processed to make its sound match the inferior sound of the other performances. And I don't know whether the Philadelphia Schubert Ninth on German AT-102 is the superior 1963 or the inferior 1976 version.

As for the performances of the later years with the NBC Symphony, in 1966 RCA Victor planned—to commemorate in 1967 the hundredth anniversary of Toscanini's birth—a reissue of the Toscanini recordings with their true sound, which was to be obtained by newly transferring without modification the sound from the original metal parts of the 78-rpm recordings or the original tapes of the LP recordings to new working tapes for the new Victrola records. I first heard about the project, in the fall of 1966, from Richard Gardner, who reported unhappily that he

[2] On the basis of my statement in parentheses on p. 23, Hall named me as one of those who had confirmed the official story, ignoring my later published denials of its truth.

had been assigned to it not to work independently, as he had always done previously, but merely to operate the controls as directed by the editor in charge of the project, a man named Zarbock; and that Zarbock, ignoring instructions, was directing him to introduce treble-boosts into the newly transferred sound. And in fact when the first group of new Victrolas appeared in 1967 the treble-boost made the violins in Debussy's *La Mer*, on VIC-1246, glistening and silky, the brass brighter and sharper— all attractive to the ear, but false. To obtain the true sound of the violins and brass one had to be able to cancel the treble-boost (with a first-class treble-control that would not also remove some of the brightness of the original sound).

Moreover, in a few instances Zarbock did not make the new transfer from the original recording; and what happened in one of these instances is worth reporting as a demonstration of how the actions of individuals behind the façade of a corporate entity can defeat that entity's intention. One morning late in October 1966 Gardner telephoned to ask me to come down to RCA Victor in the afternoon, when Zarbock and he would be making the new transfer of Beethoven's Eighth, and assured me—when I inquired—that the invitation had Zarbock's approval. Zarbock was pleasant when we met; and I took a seat facing the LC1A speaker, with Gardner at his controls and Zarbock at his desk behind me. There were three tapes, said Gardner; and the first that he played part of was a working tape made by an editor named Slick, which produced sound that was compressed, shallow and lusterless. The second, said Gardner, had nothing to identify it; but the overwhelmingly beautiful, spacious and solid sound it began to produce was unquestionably that of the original tape; and amazed and delighted I swung around toward Gardner, whom I found grinning *his* delight. We turned expectantly to Zarbock, and were dumbfounded by his grim face: he heard echo-chamber resonance, he said. Gardner and I protested that it was the natural resonance of empty Carnegie Hall; but Zarbock was adamant. Gardner then suggested that we listen to the third tape, another working tape of Slick's which produced much the same sound as the first one. Finally Zarbock consented to make a test transfer of a passage from the original tape. I heard him murmuring instructions to Gardner—the result of which was that the violins which earlier had been radiant and sweet were now strident. I said this to Zarbock, who replied that their sound had to be changed in this way on the working tape for the final record to produce what I had heard before from the original tape. I forebore to dispute this with Zarbock or to embarrass Gardner by asking if he agreed with it, and merely asked Zarbock if he would let me hear the test pressing of the record. He promised that he would, but never did; and two months later Gardner told me sadly that Zarbock—determined to have his way—had remade the Beethoven Eighth using the Slick working tape. (When I heard the record eventually it produced sound that was agreeable but without the spaciousness and lustrous beauty of the original that Slick had removed.) I reported the episode to Roger G. Hall, at that time Manager of Red Seal at Victor, and asked him to have Gardner play for him the three tapes I had heard. He did not have Gardner do this; and concerning the three tapes that he alleged were played for him he wrote that the first was the one he, like me, preferred; but that the second—only slightly different from the first, and offering better definition—was the one chosen by Zarbock for reasons as persuasive as ours for the first; and that the third was the Slick tape that all of us, including Zarbock, disliked.

Though the announced intention had been to offer on the new Victrolas the true sound of the original mono recordings for the music-lovers interested in Toscanini's performances, the Victor sales division persuaded the company to begin, early in 1968, to issue the recordings both in their original mono sound on VIC records and in "electrically reprocessed stereo" sound on VICS records for stereo-lovers, most of whom, I would have thought, would not be interested in Toscanini even in pseudo-stereo sound. The retail dealers stocked only the VICS records; and though the early Victrolas issued only in mono are available on VIC records, the later ones are available only on VICS's. (I was told that the original mono sound could be obtained from a VICS record by reducing bass 4 db in the right channel and raising the level 3 db in the left channel; but a former Victor technician was reported to have said one could recover the original mono sound merely by playing the VICS record in the mono [A + B] mode and adding a step of bass.)

The new Victrolas were issued in England first by Decca; but in 1972 RCA in England began a *Toscanini Edition* with its own remastered versions of the NBC Symphony recordings. I heard only a few that a reader lent me—the Mendelssohn *Italian* Symphony and Schubert *Unfinished* on AT-101, the Rossini overtures on AT-108, the Debussy *La Mer* and *Ibéria* on AT-111, and the Berlioz *Harold in Italy* (not reissued in the American Victrola series) on AT-112—which produced sound that was more clearly and cleanly defined in quieter aural space than that of the American Victrolas. The Debussy pieces were amazingly improved not only in this respect but in the greater spaciousness of the sound. After a couple of years, and a final group of releases that I was told were very poor, the series was terminated.

By that time German RCA had begun its *Toscanini Edition* with its own remastered versions, of which I heard only the superb-sounding Brahms Second on AT-132. From someone I considered reliable I learned that the quality of the German versions depended on the source material obtained from American RCA and what was done with it. Generally, he said, the remastering of tape material produced excellent results—e.g. the Beethoven *Pastoral* Symphony on AT-133, the Beethoven Fourth and Fifth on AT-128, the Brahms Second on AT-132, which offered the best sound my informant had ever heard—but the remastering of pre-tape (i.e. pre-1950) material produced poor results; and he remarked that "the Germans often can't leave a good-sounding tape alone," in addition to making poor material worse with bad equalization, filtering and artificial resonance.

In the following list of NBC Symphony recordings the VIC, VICS and LM numbers are those of American RCA records (the ones in parentheses designating records not available at present), and the AT numbers are those of German RCA's *Toscanini Edition*. Most of the VIC recordings, when I heard them, had the treble boosts and insufficient bass I mention, but may have been changed by now; and I suggest the procedure I followed, which was to begin the playback of a recording with treble- and bass-controls set for flat response, and then increase or decrease treble or bass as the sound required. Where I say nothing about the sound of a German recording I have received no report about it.

BACH

Air from Suite No. 3 (known as *Air for G String*). (In LM-7032.) The performance is a beautiful example of the Toscanini articulating and shaping of melody. At present it is not available.

BEETHOVEN

VIC-8000 has the nine symphonies, the *Prometheus, Egmont, Coriolan* and *Consecration of the House* Overtures, the Septet Op. 20, and the Adagio and Scherzo of the Quartet Op. 135. I discussed the sound of the Symphony No. 8 earlier; as for the others, some of the defects in recording were ineradicable, but except for the treble boosts—in Nos. 1, 3, 6 and 7, the second movements of Nos. 2, 4 and 5, and the third movement of No. 9—these were the best-sounding of all the versions issued. The sound of the Septet was excellent; the *Egmont* needed reduction of treble; the quartet movements were improved by reducing treble and adding bass, the *Coriolan* and *Consecration* by adding treble and bass.

Except for the Ninth on VIC-1607 the symphonies are available singly only on VICS records.

AT-600 has all nine symphonies; AT-117 has Nos. 1 and 2; AT-121 No. 3 *(Eroica)*; AT-128 Nos. 4 and 5; AT-133 No. 6 *(Pastoral)*; AT-140 Nos. 7 and 8; AT-143 No. 9. The sound of Nos. 3 and 6 was reported to be the best produced from their tapes; that of Nos. 4 and 5 to be good; that of No. 9 to be poor. AT-136 has the overtures in VIC-8000, with the *Fidelio* and *Leonore No. 3*; AT-144 the Septet and the quartet movements.

Of the performances of the Piano Concertos No. 1 with Ania Dorfmann (LM-1039), No. 3 with Rubinstein (RCA LCT-1009) and No. 4 with Serkin (VIC-1521), which are worth acquiring only for Toscanini's enlivening of the orchestral parts, AT-106 has Nos. 1 and 4.

The performance of *Fidelio* on LM-6025 has Rose Bampton's

monotonously shrill Leonore, Herbert Janssen's rough-voiced Pizzaro, Sidor Belarsky's bad pronunciation of German in the role of Rocco, but Eleanor Steber's beautiful singing as Marzelline and Jan Peerce's excellent Florestan; however the flawed singing is made negligible by Toscanini's uniquely great pacing and shaping of the work. And the same may be said of the flawed and "enhanced" sound from the recording that is a transfer from (1) the acetate discs of NBC's recording of the broadcasts of 10 and 17 December 1944, (2) the recording of "*Abscheulicher! wo eilst du hin?*" made after the broadcasts, and (3) the 1945 recording of the *Leonore No. 3* Overture.

The *Fidelio* on AT-204 has been reported to have better sound.

As in the finale of the Ninth, Toscanini's unfailing sense for continuity and coherence integrates the many sections of the *Missa Solemnis* into a unified progression from one sublimity to the next; and equally overwhelming is his realization of the mystically rapt opening sections of the *Sanctus* and the *Benedictus*, the radiant *allegretto* section of the *Agnus Dei*. The performance (LM-6013) had excellent singing by Lois Marshall, Nan Merriman, Eugene Conley, Jerome Hines and the Robert Shaw Chorale; and the sound was good; but poor microphone-placement made the chorus predominate over soloists and orchestra.

The *Missa Solemnis* is also on AT-200.

BERLIOZ

It was the mercurial finale in a Toscanini performance of *Harold in Italy* around 1930 that had me following the operation of the Berlioz mind with new understanding and delight. The performance—unequalled by any other I have heard—owed its effectiveness largely to its accuracy in tempo. Toscanini once pointed out to me the necessity of obeying the metronome markings that Koussevitzky, for one, grandly ignored: the tempos they prescribed integrated not only the sections of a movement—notably the third movement—but the movements within the entire work, and made the recurring viola melody move at the same pace in each movement. The fine-sounding performance (LM-

1951) derived from the broadcast of 29 November 1953 is on AT-112.

In 1947, when Toscanini conducted the broadcast performance of the entire *Romeo and Juliet* from which the recording (LM-7034) was processed, he could say "I am the only one who conduct this work;" and after Munch and Monteux had recorded it he might have said he was the only one who performed it in the tempos prescribed by Berlioz that gave it correct shape and expressive effect. Thus in the *Love Scene* the *"premiers transports, premiers aveux, premiers serments"* are embodied in musical terms of the most exquisite delicacy, which not only characterize the emotions of the young lovers but convey the delicacy of feeling of Berlioz himself—terms which include a recurring wistful phrase of the violins; and played by Toscanini in the tempo Berlioz prescribed, the phrase communicated the delicate feeling Berlioz intended; whereas slowed down by other conductors it was sentimentalized. The performance is on AT-206, presumably with sound as good as on LM-7034.

The superb performance of the *Roman Carnival* Overture on VIC-1244 required volume to be increased at the beginning of the *allegro* portion. This may be true also of the transfer on AT-100.

BIZET

The superb performance of the Suite from *Carmen* is on VIC-1263 with excellent sound which needed additional bass, and on AT-109 with sound reported to be poor.

BRAHMS

VIC-6400 has the four symphonies, the *Variations on a Theme of Haydn* and the *Tragic* and *Academic Festival Overtures*, with excellent sound requiring only reduction of treble.

AT-115 has the Symphony No. 1, AT-132 No. 2, AT-146 No. 4, all with the best sound my informant had ever heard; but he reported the sound of No. 3 on AT-137 to be poor.

AT-125 has the *Variations on a Theme of Haydn* and the

Concerto for Violin and Cello with Mischa Mischakoff and Frank Miller.

At-152 has the *Tragic* and *Academic Festival Overtures* and the boring Serenade in A.

The Piano Concerto No. 2 with Horowitz is on RCA ARM1-2874 and AT-103.

CHERUBINI

The broadcast performance of the *Requiem* in C minor (LM-2000), with excellent sound that required reduction of treble, is on AT-147.

The performances of the Symphony in D (LM-1745) and the Overtures to *Ali Baba,, Anacreon* and *Medea* (LM-7026) are on AT-135.

DEBUSSY

I spoke earlier of the beautiful sound of the *Ibéria* and *La Mer* on VIC-1246, except for the treble boost in *La Mer* that requires reduction of treble; and of their even more beautiful sound on the English AT-111, which leads me to believe that their sound on the German AT-111 may also be more beautiful.

DUKAS

The performance of *The Sorcerer's Apprentice* is on VIC-1267 with Strauss tone poems.

DVORAK

The beautiful-sounding performance of the Symphony No. 9 *(From the New World)* on VIC-1249 that made the work "as fresh and glistening as creation itself" is now listed only on VICS-1249. And its sound on AT-114 has been reported to be poor.

ELGAR

The superb performance of the *Enigma Variations* is listed only on VICS-1344.

FRANCK

The beautiful sound of the performance of *Psyche and Eros* on VIC-1245 (with Debussy's *Ibéria* and *La Mer*) required reduction of treble and increase of bass.

GERSHWIN

It is amazing to hear in the performance of *An American in Paris* reissued on RCA AVM1-1737 what—with his feeling for shape of phrase, his grace and rubato, in the playing of melody—Toscanini made of the piece and its blues. It is also on AT-129.

GLUCK

The superb broadcast performance of Act 2 of *Orfeo ed Euridice* with Nan Merriman, Barbara Gibson and the Robert Shaw Chorale had flawed sound (LM-1850 and LVT-1041), which it may also have on AT-127.

HAYDN

VIC-1262 has the superb performance of the Symphony No. 101 *(Clock)*, no longer blurred by the echo-chamber resonance that was added to conceal the acoustic deadness of Studio 3A. The first two movements have what appears to be the spacious and solid sound of the original 78-rpm recording, with its surface noise; the last two the thin, shallow sound and quiet surface of the LP transfer. The reverse side has the Symphony No. 94 *(Surprise)*, with the Minuet played in an *Allegro molto* tempo too fast for the articulation and sense of the music, and the fast tempos of the first and last movements maintained too rigidly. Its excellent sound required reduction of treble and increase of bass. The performances are also on AT-120.

The superb performance of No. 88 (RCA LCT-7) is on AT-130 with the New York Philharmonic No. 101. The sound is reported to be poor.

AT-149 has superb broadcast performances of No. 99 and the less interesting Sinfonia Concertante Op. 84.

MENDELSSOHN

The enchanting performance of the incidental music for *A Midsummer Night's Dream,* originally recorded with insufficient brightness, is listed only on VICS-1337. Its sound on AT-138 is reported to need increased treble and reduced bass.

The superb broadcast performance of the Symphony No. 4 *(Italian)* (VIC-1341) needed additional bass in the first, third and fourth movements, and reduced treble in the second and third. It is available on AT-101.

AT-123 has the performance of the less interesting Symphony No. 5 *(Reformation)* (LM-1851).

The elegantly impassioned broadcast performance of the Octet for Strings (LM-1869) had good sound in the first two movements, harsher sound in the third, and strident tuttis in the finale.

MOZART

(VIC-1330) had the impassioned and dramatic performance of the Symphony K.550 in G minor and a performance of the Symphony K.543 whose second and third movements were much too fast, with sound that required reduction of treble and increase of bass.

The performance of the Symphony K.385 *(Haffner)* (LM-1038) had sound that was unpleasant in its extreme acoustical deadness and its sharpness, and that later was made worse by blurring "enhancement".

The performance of the Symphony K.551 (known as *Jupiter)* (LM-1030) offered the first movement with all its majesty and radiance, and a beautiful realization of the Minuet; but in the second movement Toscanini's *Andante cantabile* tempo in terms of the 3/4 time signature became too fast in the passages of thirty-second notes; and the faster-than-usual finale was blurred by reverberation. The later "enhanced" version produced blurred sound.

Toscanini's enlivening inflection of the orchestral part in the performance of the Bassoon Concerto K.191 with Leonard Sharrow (LM-1030) made it delightful; and the sound was excellent.

The superb performance of the Divertimento K.287 for Horns

and Strings (LM-13) had good sound which later (LM-2001) was beefed up by treble and bass boosts.

The performances of the Overtures to *The Marriage of Figaro*, *Don Giovanni* and *The Magic Flute* (LM-7026) had good sound.

AT-110 has the symphonies K.550 in G minor and K.551; AT-126 the Symphonies K.385 *(Haffner)* and K.543; AT-141 the Divertimento K.287 and the Bassoon Concerto K.191; AT-116, whose sound is reported to be poor, has the Overture to *Figaro*; AT-134, whose sound is reported to be very poor, has the Overtures to *The Magic Flute* and *Don Giovanni*.

MUSORGSKY

The superb performance of Ravel's transcription of *Pictures at an Exhibition* is on VIC-1273 with the same extreme treble boost that damaged it when it was first issued, making drastic reduction of treble necessary; and is also on AT-107.

PROKOFIEV

Koussevitzky's performances of the first and last movements of the *Classical Symphony* were successions of miraculous sonorities that constituted one of the wonders of the age. But the clear texture of strands of sound excitingly enlivened by Toscanini's sharp inflection (LM-9020) seemed to me the correct treatment of the music. On the other hand his strict obedience to the *Larghetto* prescribed for the second movement made it too slow. The sound was excellent. The performance is also on AT-122.

PUCCINI

The definitive performance of *La Bohème* derived from NBC recordings of the broadcasts of 3 and 10 February 1946—with Licia Albanese, Ann McKnight, Jan Peerce and Francesco Valentino—is listed only on VICS-6019, and is also on AT-203.

RAVEL

The Suite No. 2 from *Daphnis et Chloé* is on VIC-1273 with good sound that required reduction of treble. It is also on AT-107.

RESPIGHI

VIC-1244 has *Fountains* and *Pines of Rome* in good sound that needed reduction of treble and addition of bass. They are also on AT-100.

ROSSINI

Toscanini's unique performances of the Overtures to *L'Italiana in Algeri*, *La Cenerentola* and *The Siege of Corinth* are on VIC-1248 in good sound; and VIC-1274 has the Overtures to *Semiramide* (add bass, reduce treble) and *William Tell* (reduce treble), with good transfers of the 78-rpm Overtures to *The Barber of Seville*, *La Gazza Ladra* and *Il Signor Bruschino* and the *Passo a sei* from *William Tell* (increase treble for all, bass for the first two).

AT-108, which has the Overtures to *The Barber of Seville*, *Il Signor Bruschino*, *La Gazza Ladra* and *William Tell*; AT-116, which has the Overture to *L'Italiana in Algeri*; and AT-109, which has the *Passo a sei* from *William Tell*, all are reported to have poor sound.

SAINT-SAËNS

The broadcast performance of the Symphony No. 3 (LM-1869) is on AT-150 with sound that is reported to be poor.

SCHUBERT

The early Symphony No. 5, which is made delightful by the lightness and delicacy, the grace and lilt, the beautiful modeling of Toscanini's performance, and the *Unfinished* No. 8 are on VIC-1311 with sound that needed reduction of treble in both and addition of bass to the second movement of No. 8.

The tremendous performance of No. 9 (LM-1835) required reduction of treble and bass.

No. 5 is on AT-123; No. 8 on AT-101; and No. 9 on AT-151.

SCHUMANN

I heard only part of the recording (LM-2048) of the broadcast performance of the Symphony No. 3 *(Rhenish)*, which reproduced it with strident sound. Its sound on AT-138 is reported to be not strident but airless, requiring reduction of treble and addition of bass.

The first half of the impassioned and beautifully shaped performance of the *Manfred* Overture on VIC-1249 required reduction of treble and addition of bass; the rest, brightening with increased treble. It is listed now only on VICS-1249.

SIBELIUS

The freshly conceived, excitingly effective broadcast performance of the Symphony No. 2 (LM-6711) is on AT-139.

SMETANA

The genial and engaging performance of the attractive *Die Moldau* is on VIC-1245 with good sound that needed reduction of treble and addition of bass. An uncharacteristic discontinuity in the transition from the first section to the second appears to be the result of a splicing of parts of two performances.

STRAUSS, RICHARD

VIC-1267 has an accurate and plastically coherent performance of *Don Juan* that is more effective than the usual underlining of every point, and a marvelously clarifying performance of *Till Eulenspiegel*, both in excellent sound that required only reduction of treble.

Don Quixote, Strauss's orchestral masterpiece, was excellently reproduced by the recording (LM-2026) of the performance with Frank Miller derived from the 1953 broadcast, which was marvelous in its clarity of densely woven texture, its plastic coherence, its expressive point. It is available on AT-148.

The superb performance of *Death and Transfiguration* (LM-1891) is available, with *Till Eulenspiegel*, on AT-105.

TCHAIKOVSKY

By playing the Symphony No. 6 (*Pathétique*) exactly as the score directs, with none of the traditional distorting overemphasis, Toscanini restores its organic coherence, its expressive force and its artistic validity. The transfer of the airless and lusterless 78-rpm sound on VIC-1268 needed brightening with additional treble, and additional bass in the second half of the finale; also it was noisy, and the first half of the finale was murky. It is also available on AT-104.

The sound of the superb performance of the *Manfred* Symphony on VIC-1315 needed reduction of treble in the third movement and latter part of the finale. It is now listed only on VICS-1315; and its sound on AT-145 is reported to be poor.

The transfer of the 78-rpm sound of *Romeo and Juliet* on VIC-1245 needed increased treble and bass. And its sound on AT-119 is reported to be damaged by echo-chamber resonance.

The sound of the superb performance of the *Nutcracker Suite* on VIC-1263, with treble reduced and bass increased, was excellent; and its sound on AT-119 is reported to be good.

The bad sound of the electrifying 1941 performance of the Piano Concerto No. 1 (with Horowitz) on VIC-1554 made it one to avoid, and the 1943 performance on LM-2319 the one to acquire. I don't know which performance is on AT-113.

VERDI

The most accurately, beautifully and effectively shaped performance of *Aida* on records, derived from the broadcasts of 26 March and 2 April 1949—with Herva Nelli, Eva Gustafson, Richard Tucker and Giuseppe Valdengo—whose 8H sound on VIC-6113 needed reduction of treble and increase of bass, is now listed only on VICS-6113. It is also on AT-302.

The performance of *Un Ballo in Maschera* (LM-6112) derived from the broadcasts of 17 and 24 January 1954—with excellent singing by Nelli, Claramae Turner and Jan Peerce, but not by Robert Merrill—had spacious Carnegie Hall sound that lacked warmth. It is available now on AT-300.

The performance of *Falstaff* derived from the broadcasts of 1 and 8 April 1950—with excellent singing by Valdengo, Frank Guarrera, Nelli, Merriman, Chloë Elmo and Teresa Stich-Randall—is on LM-6111 with sound which needed reduction of treble and bass, and in which vocal parts that were sung *piano* and *pianissimo* were reproduced *forte* and blanketed the orchestral part. It is available also on AT-301.

The incandescent and as yet unequalled performance of *Otello* (LM-6107) derived from the broadcasts of 1 and 8 December 1947—with excellent singing by Ramon Vinay, Nelli and Valdengo—had "enhanced" 8H sound which falsified the voices and which reverberated through endless empty halls. Its sound on AT-303 has been reported by one reader to be good, and by another reader to have treble and bass boosts that make it thinner and shriller than on LM-6107.

The definitive performance of *La Traviata* derived from the broadcasts of 1 and 8 December 1946, with for the most part excellent singing by Albanese and Peerce, is on LM-6003—its 8H sound flat, shallow and at times harsh. It is also available on AT-202.

The superb performances of Act 4 of *Rigoletto* with Zinka Milanov, Peerce and Leonard Warren in their prime; the Trio from Act 3 of *I Lombardi* with Vivian Della Chiesa, Peerce and Nicola Moscona; and the Overture and aria "*Quando le sere al placido*" from *Luisa Miller* (VIC-1314) all required additional treble; and the first needed additional bass.

The superb performance with the Shaw Chorale of the *Te Deum*, possibly Verdi's most heart-piercingly beautiful single piece of writing, needed (VIC-1331) reduction of treble and additional bass; the chorus of the Hebrew slaves from *Nabucco* needed additional bass; the *Hymn of the Nations* needed reduction of treble. They are listed now only on VICS-1331; and their sound on AT-131 is reported to be poor.

The performances of the Overture to *I Vespri Siciliani* and Preludes to Acts 1 and 3 of *La Traviata* on VIC-1248—but not the Overture to *La Forza del Destino*—needed reduction of treble and addition of bass.

The material from the preceding three records assembled in AT-304, *Verdi and Toscanini*, is reported to have very poor sound.

The performance of the *Requiem* on LM-6018—with Nelli, Fedora Barbieri, Giuseppe Di Stefano, Cesare Siepi and the Shaw Chorale—is a piecing together, by Gardner and Toscanini, of parts of the tapes of the broadcast of 27 January 1951 and its dress rehearsal; and it is a grim sort of joke on Toscanini that after all this work he approved a performance in which Nelli (presumably at an earlier rehearsal) doesn't sing her last *"Libera me"* seventeen measures from the end. The excellent sound varied throughout in balance, solidity and other characteristics. The performance is also on AT-201.

WAGNER

Of the pieces on VIC-1247, the Prelude to Act 1 of *Die Meistersinger* needed no change; but the Prelude to Act 3 and the Preludes to Acts 1 and 3 of *Lohengrin* required reduction of treble and increase of bass; the *Siegfried-Idyll* reduction of treble; the *Faust Overture* reduction of treble at the beginning, but increase of treble toward the end.

The performances of the Prelude and Finale of *Tristan und Isolde* and the Prelude and *Good Friday Spell* of *Parsifal* on VIC-1278 needed reduction of treble and increase of bass.

The overwhelming performance of *Siegfried's Death and Funeral Music* from *Die Götterdämmerung* (VIC-1316) needed reduction of treble and increase of bass; the broadcast performance of the last scene of Act 1 of *Die Walküre*, which provides a marvelously shaped orchestral context for not very good singing by Helen Traubel and Lauritz Melchior, needed reduction of treble. They are listed now only on VICS-1316.

VIC-1369 has the excellently reproduced 1941 performance of the *Immolation Scene* from *Die Götterdämmerung*, with Traubel at her best, that delighted Toscanini, and the 1941 broadcast performance of music from Act 1—the instrumental *Dawn and Rhine Journey* that Toscanini performed frequently, with, this time, the Brünnhilde-Siegfried duet sung by Traubel and Melchior.

The material from the preceding records assembled in AT-400, *Wagner and Toscanini*, is reported to have poor sound.

WEBER

Of the excellent performances of the Overtures to *Euryanthe*, *Oberon* and *Der Freischütz* (VIC-1341), the last two needed additional bass.

COLLECTIONS

Listed now only on VICS-1321 is the collection *Invitation to the Dance* (VIC-1321), with a number of Toscanini's enchanting performances of light and "pop" music: Waldteufel's *Skaters Waltz*, Strauss's *Blue Danube Waltz* and *Tritsch-Tratsch Polka*, Paganini's *Moto Perpetuo*, Berlioz's *Rakoczy March*, the Weber-Berlioz *Invitation to the Dance* and the *Ballabili* from Verdi's *Otello*. The Paganini piece and Strauss Polka exhibit the extraordinary energy and fire in the operation of conductor and orchestra in the first NBC years. The first four pieces needed additional bass and treble; the *Rakoczy March* only additionl bass; the last two pieces additional bass and reduced treble.

The collection with the same title on AT-118 has the Waldteufel and Strauss pieces and the Weber-Berlioz *Invitation to the Dance*, with a few Brahms *Hungarian Dances* and the *Waltz of the Flowers* from Tchaikovsky's *Nutcracker Suite*, in sound that is reported to be poor.

The enchanting performance of *Dance of the Hours* from Ponchielli's *La Gioconda* is on VIC-1263 with the suite from Bizet's *Carmen* and Tchaikovsky's *Nutcracker Suite*.

The overtures of Cherubini, Mozart and Rossini in the collection *Toscanini Plays Overtures* (LM-7026) are listed earlier under the names of their composers.

The collections of overtures of operas on AT-116 and AT-134, dances from operas on AT-109, and concert favorites on AT-124 are reported to have poor sound.

6

THE WRITING ABOUT TOSCANINI

The writing about Toscanini brings to mind the statement by Goethe that Randall Jarrell quoted once—that "in the face of the great superiority of another person there is no safety but love"—which must be qualified, it seems to me, by the fact that some, when faced by this superiority, find safety in envy, resentment, hate—the hate, a friend remarked, of the untalented for the talented.

Thus, it was not the NBC Symphony musicians who *loved* Toscanini that Jerome Toobin—in his book *Agitato* about his experiences as manager of the Symphony of the Air—quoted on the subject of Toscanini's walking out at rehearsals, but rather those he chose to call "iconoclastic orchestra men", who told him that "Toscanini's dramatic walkouts came generally when he was bored with a rehearsal"—"an eventuality," Toobin added, "which happened occasionally even to that titan." With confidence justified—as Toobin's was not—by what I observed at the rehearsals and what the musicians I talked to said about them, I maintain that the boredom Toobin said happened occasionally was one thing that never happened: Toscanini, rehearsing a piece of music, was never less than completely and intensely involved; this involvement occasionally caused him to explode in anger when he felt that the orchestra was not as intensely involved as he; and this anger born of frustration could, on such occasions, attain an extreme that impelled him to walk out.

Writing that it had never been ascertained to his satisfaction why Toscanini hadn't given the Symphony of the Air any support in its fight for survival, Toobin cited two explanations that had been offered. On the one hand, "Some say [Toscanini] was kept from knowing the facts of the [orchestra's] struggle by his son, Walter," which one could have expected Toobin—from what the men of the orchestra must have told him about the "entourage's" protective wall around Toscanini—to know was the true explanation. But he was impressed instead by the view, on the other hand, of "the astute, sophisticated Erich Leinsdorf", who claimed to have been told by old-timers (unnamed) that Toscanini "thought the Met should fold after he left it [in 1915]. And he thought the Philharmonic should go out of business after he left in 1936. And he never conceded that there even *was* a La Scala when he wasn't there. So how do you think he must feel about an orchestra that was *his* in the fullest sense of the word. I wouldn't expect too much from the Toscaninis." All seemingly "astute and sophisticated", and especially so to Toobin, who quoted it, he said, "because in essence I ascribe to Leinsdorf's view. After all, no one ever questioned Toscanini's great ego, and who, in God's name, ever had more reason for self-esteem in his work?" Plausible, but actually as remote from reality as Leinsdorf's allegations. What Toscanini told me (see p. 79) about his leaving the Metropolitan, what he told me (pp. 79-80) about his resignation from La Scala, what he told Dusolina Giannini who told me (p. 50) about his leaving the Philharmonic—all confirmed in the Sachs biography—revealed no such expectation of their dying without him as Leinsdorf asserted. And not only did NBC musicians report his grief and rage over the disbanding of "my poor orchestra", but Toobin himself mentioned on p. 87 of his book "the well-known fact that Toscanini had hoped Cantelli would succeed him as conductor of the NBC Symphony." As for the great ego that Toobin said no one ever questioned, I do question it as one who never saw a sign of it in my contacts with him; and the NBC musicians I knew who were closely involved with him for so many years spoke only about his humility and about what Sachs terms his "relentless self-dissatisfaction".

In addition to these inventions of Leinsdorf's to demonstrate his astuteness and sophistication, there were those of the musical journalists to demonstrate their perception and understanding—which actually most of them lacked. Whereas in Toscanini's lifetime the way to impress one's readers was to admire him, in recent years it has been to attack him—in writing that, whether

in admiration or attack, most often represented not perception
but invention. Or—with even more impressive effect—the writing
has discriminated judiciously between invented strengths and
weaknesses, achievements and failures. This pseudo-discrim-
ination in Marsh's book won it predictable praise for its "ob-
jectivity", its "freedom from piety, hero worship . . . and
legend-building". Nor is Marsh its only practitioner. In an article
by Irving Kolodin about *The Meaning of Toscanini*, some years
ago, one read, among other such pronouncements, that "Toscanini, superior as he is to the common mold, is yet within it. For a
stiff 'Magic Flute' Overture there is a superbly flexible 'Freischütz,' for an overwrought 'Leonore No. 3' a wonderfully pro-
clamatory 'Meistersinger'." And there is Alan Rich, who on
Station KPFA in San Francisco 25 years ago, when I first heard
of him, was getting the attention he wanted with his attacks on
the "Toscanini myth" and references to "Saint Arturo", to
which he added—in a letter to a questioner of this method of
evaluating Toscanini's performances—that he found in their
over-expository treatment of the music, which made it harsh and
unbeautiful, evidence of Toscanini's lack of musical culture. By
now the Rich performance has changed: in an article in *New
York* magazine which used the Sachs biography as a mere point
of departure for his customary airing of his own lurid inventions,
Rich now talked about a Toscanini in whom he recognized "the
fabulous command the man had over players, the unique values
he could isolate in the music he truly understood," but insisted
on recognition also that this man "never could draw a Mozartean singing line out of an orchestra;" that for all his alleged
dedication to "fidelity to the composer's wishes" he performed
Respighi's orchestral arrangements of Bach; that he inflicted a
Herva Nelli or a Jan Peerce on the operas of Verdi—in sum, that
it was "this imperfect aesthete, this sometime vulgarian" who
"[created] in music a standard of performance that—veiled in
legend and insane hype though it may be—stands on a peak that
will never again be scaled." But Toscanini's failure to perceive
how unsuited Respighi's style of orchestration was to Bach has
no bearing on the different and essential matter of his fidelity to
the directions for the performance of their works that Mozart,
Haydn, Beethoven, Schubert, Berlioz, Tchaikovsky and the rest

provided in their scores. Also, I hear in the Andante of Mozart's Divertimento K. 287, as elsewhere, the Mozartean singing line Rich said Toscanini was incapable of obtaining from an orchestra; and in the Verdi operas the admirable singing by Nelli and Peerce that Rich thought Toscanini should have recognized as inadmissible there.

Toscanini's alleged "fidelity to the composer's wishes"—part of the "legend and insane hype" Rich referred to—he described as "one of the Toscanini catchphrases . . . used to depict Toscanini as some sort of super-Laundromat in which begrimed scores could be returned to pristine whiteness." This he characterized as nonsense: "On rehearsal tapes you constantly hear him tinkering," he said, citing the *sostenuto,* not prescribed in the score of Beethoven's *Coriolan* Overture, that Toscanini introduced in four bars near the end of the exposition. And Toscanini's recorded *Traviata* was proof that "even in Italian opera he was as willing as the next man to betray the composer by traditional cuts." But the undistorted meaning of Toscanini's "fidelity to the composer's wishes" was what Rich himself described—in a New York *Herald Tribune* article in 1964 on the Toscanini Memorial Archive of microfilms of original manuscripts—as "the pursuit of musical correctitude . . . [the] clearing away [of] the debris of editorial corruption in printed scores to get at the composer's original design"—i.e. the design indicated by his original musical notes and his original markings for their performance, which were what Toscanini constantly worried about at rehearsals. With these established, there were then the inflections of phrasing that Toscanini understood it to be the performer's task to fill in between Mozart's or Beethoven's marking of *piano* at one point and of *forte* eight bars later. And only rarely, impelled by what he felt to be required by the music, did he go beyond this—as in his distention of the climactic four unison Cs in the coda of the finale of Schubert's C-major Symphony, in the Philadelphia Orchestra performance, and the similar *sostenuto,* for climactic force, of the reiterated rhythmic figure in the four bars of the *Coriolan* Overture that Rich cited. As for cuts in opera, I believe they were limited to the two in *La Traviata*—of the second stanza of Violetta's *"Ah, fors' è lui"* and the traditional cabaletta of Alfredo's *"De' miei bollenti spiriti"*—which don't

seem to me a sufficient basis for a generalization about Toscanini's willingness to betray the composer.

After all these fictional "ego trips" one is grateful for the book
in which Sachs is content to set down what his years of research
established as the facts of the life and work of a musical genius
who, it turns out, was a man of great personal decency and gener-
osity. It is a book for those who have been moved by their contacts with the musical genius, and will find themselves moved by
what they will learn about the man. And for those who will read
it I add a few details that it doesn't include.

Sachs mentions the first meeting of Toscanini and Furtwängler in Milan in 1923, when Furtwängler conducted the
Scala Orchestra in two concerts, and Toscanini, after one of the
rehearsals, rushed to him and shook his hand warmly. But he says
nothing about their next encounter the following year in Zürich,
where Toscanini conducted his orchestra in Brahms's Symphony
No. 2. Rudolf Serkin, for whom the performance was an "in-
credible revelation", has described how Furtwängler, at a private
reception after the concert, "embarrassingly and painfully told
Toscanini in violent terms what he thought" about some things
in the performance, while Toscanini listened "like a little boy",
and then replied: "When Steinbach [the conductor contemporary with Brahms whose performances of Brahms's symphonies
were considered authoritative] came to Turin and conducted the
Brahms Second Symphony, after the first rehearsal he turned to
the orchestra and said: 'I have nothing to do. Who is your conductor?' And the answer was 'Toscanini'." The two incidents
demonstrate the contrasting responses of Toscanini and Furtwängler to the achievements of others, confirming the statement
by Hugo Burghauser of the Vienna Philharmonic about the be-
nevolence Furtwängler exhibited toward lesser conductors but
not toward the eminent ones whom he regarded as rivals.

That attitude of Furtwängler played a part in the next incident, which Sachs describes inadequately in the statement
"Furtwängler, who had been very successful in his guest appearances with the [New York] Philharmonic, began to lose support with the orchestra's management soon after Toscanini's
arrival." Furtwängler's first guest engagement in January 1925
had been a series of triumphs with orchestra, public and press
that had led the management to engage him for two months of

each of the following two seasons. Arriving in February 1926, after Toscanini's first guest engagement, and expecting a repetition of his triumphs of the previous year, he encountered instead the lessened responses of an orchestra, a public and a press still overwhelmed by the performances conducted by Toscanini. This disappointing and humiliating failure he regarded—since he could think of others only as being motivated by the same vanity and jealousy as his own—as having been contrived somehow by Toscanini—especially since his lessened box-office appeal eventually caused the management not to re-engage him as it did Toscanini.

Sachs does report Furtwängler's accusation in 1927 that Toscanini had demanded and been given the performance of Beethoven's Ninth originally assigned to himself, and cites the documentary evidence that Toscanini's performance of the Ninth had been arranged in 1926 at a time when Furtwängler had not even submitted any suggestions for his own 1927 programs. And he mentions that Toscanini, on the other hand, when he resigned from the Philharmonic in 1936, recommended Furtwängler as his successor. But concerning the final eposide in Salzburg in 1937 his statement—that Furtwängler insisted on talking with Toscanini about the possibility of his conducting Der Freischütz in Salzburg in 1938, and was told by Toscanini that he could conduct whatever he wanted, but Toscanini would not be there—is again inadequate.

According to Sachs's informant, Burghauser, the Vienna Philharmonic's chairman at that time, Furtwängler had declined repeated invitations to conduct at the Salzburg Festival; and it was only when Toscanini's activity had made the festival a center of international prestige and publicity that Furtwängler, in 1937, presented his claim as a German musician to participation in a festival on German soil, suggesting that he conduct a German opera, Der Freischütz, there in 1938. The festival's Administrative Director, Kerber, replied that his conducting of opera was a matter for Toscanini to decide, but the administration could include Furtwängler among the guests who were to conduct concerts that summer. With the matter of opera left to be taken up with Toscanini, Furtwängler accepted the offer of 27 August for a performance of Beethoven's Ninth. He was in Salzburg before that date, attending a rehearsal of Toscanini's and the concert;

and he could have talked with Toscanini on one of his free days in that period; but instead he chose to speak to him in the intermission of Toscanini's performance of *Fidelio* on 26 August, and requested that Burghauser take him to Toscanini's dressing room. Appalled, Burghauser tried to dissuade him by describing the scene in the dressing room: Toscanini on a chair, stripped to the waist, the sweat running down his body; his wife drying him and spraying him with eau de cologne while he fanned himself and perhaps refreshed himself with a few grapes. It was clearly a time to leave Toscanini undisturbed; but Furtwängler insisted, and Burghauser finally had to give in. At his pre-arranged knock Signora Toscanini opened the door slightly, and seeing him opened it wider; whereupon Furtwängler pushed past her into the room and stood towering over Toscanini, who peered up at him, not recognizing him at first.

"I wish to speak to you about my future participation in Salzburg," said Furtwängler.

Toscanini, though still dazed, managed to answer: "We speak tomorrow—after Ninth Symphony." And Furtwängler left.

Toscanini attended the performance of the Ninth, feeling that this courtesy was required of him. At his villa afterwards he told Furtwängler he had not liked the performance; and then the exchange occurred that Sachs reports. The reason for Toscanini's statement—that Furtwängler might, if he wished, conduct opera in Salzburg, but not in Toscanini's company—was the difference he saw between his own conducting in Fascist Italy and Furtwängler's conducting in Nazi Germany. Toscanini had conducted in Italy as if the Fascist régime didn't exist; Furtwängler claimed to have acted in the same way, but his claim was false.

One other fact that Sachs doesn't say enough about is that, according to Burghauser, the lessened response Furtwängler experienced when he followed Toscanini in New York in 1926 was experienced also by the greatly admired conductors—Walter, Kleiber, Busch, Krauss, Weingartner—who followed him in Vienna in the '30s. They were bewildered and reduced to despair; and Krauss and Weingartner even resorted to behind-the-scene moves against Toscanini. The Philharmonic hadn't expected all this, and recognized that it was unfortunate and unjust, but could do nothing to prevent it.

APPENDIX

The following article by B. H. Haggin appeared in *Tri-Quarterly* magazine, Winter 1966-67, under the title *Genius Betrayed*.

In his biography of David Sarnoff, Eugene Lyons writes about Sarnoff's efforts on behalf of high-quality music on the air, which he says attained their climax in Toscanini's broadcasts with the NBC Symphony. "In *Toscanini, an Intimate Portrait*, a charming and colorful little book published in 1956, the late Samuel Chotzinoff told how it all started," says Lyons. But Chotzinoff's account—of his trip to Milan in 1937 for NBC; of Mme. Toscanini's "No, no ... *impossibile*" concerning the NBC proposal, her warning about Toscanini's "current state of unreceptiveness", her advice to "wait for some more propitious moment;" of the days and weeks passing, with Chotzinoff not daring to speak and Toscanini getting impatient at his silence; of the visit of the Gatti-Casazzas during which Toscanini recalled to Gatti the man with the evil eye who had ruined the premiere of *Euryanthe* at the Metropolitan; of Chotzinoff's staying on after the Gattis left and his taking advantage of Toscanini's good humor to bring up the NBC proposal; of his persuading Toscanini to accept it by telling him a story about some canaries that had begun to sing in the choral finale of Beethoven's Ninth during the broadcast of a Toscanini performance with the New York Philharmonic—all this, while certainly colorful, is, I am sure, mostly untrue. The January 1938 issue of *Fortune* had an article about the newly initiated NBC Symphony broadcasts written by friends of Chotzinoff, Russell and Marcia Davenport, which included an account of the Milan negotiations that he must have given when he returned: that he had cabled Toscanini in advance that he was coming with an "important proposition"; that at his first meeting with the Toscaninis he wasn't able to nerve himself to answer their questions about the "proposition"; that the next day he first consulted Mme. Toscanini, who thought Toscanini would be not annoyed but interested; that Chotzinoff thereupon did give Toscanini NBC's invitation and the memorandum outlining several alternative offers; and that after reading the memorandum carefully Toscanini accepted the offer of a series of ten weekly broadcasts. In addition to the other good reasons for believing the account in *Fortune* rather than the one in Chotzinoff's book eighteen years later, there is the fact that Lyons supplies the date of Toscanini's acceptance, 2 February 1937, and the *Fortune* article begins: "It was the last day of January, 1937, and rain and sleet shrouded the boat train as it pulled into the big, drafty station at Milan."

If one asks why Chotzinoff should have invented those details eighteen years later, part of the answer is that he did it for the same reason as he invented the details in his account of the terrible incident near the end of the *Tannhäuser* Bacchanale, in the last broadcast in 1954, when Toscanini's memory failed him and he stopped conducting, putting his hand to his eyes in an attempt to remember. What actually happened at that point was that the orchestra's first cellist, Frank Miller, kept the performance going, Toscanini began to beat time again, the piece was completed, and the audience applauded. But Chotzinoff writes in his book that when Toscanini stopped conducting "the men stopped playing and the house was engulfed in terrible silence;" and his reason for writing what isn't true is that it makes a more dramatic story. This, I repeat, is also one of his reasons for the inventions about the negotiations in Milan; but in these he has an additional purpose. The purpose is evident in the picture of Toscanini that is presented: the Toscanini who in the *Fortune* account behaves wholly reasonably and rationally is transformed in the book into someone whose moods terrorize everyone around him, who tells a story about a man with the evil eye, and who is persuaded to accept NBC's offer by a story about canaries having joined in his broadcast of the Ninth. The purpose is fully achieved in the many additional stories in the book with which Chotzinoff—professing to write as a long-suffering but still devoted friend revealing the human weaknesses of a fascinating genius—horrified a public which had heard of Toscanini's explosions at rehearsals, but only now learned of the extremes to which, according to Chotzinoff, he carried the abuse of his power and privileges, in his professional and personal dealings with others. I am unable to say that everything Chotzinoff writes in the book is untrue; and I am far from contending that Toscanini was not a difficult person; but what I do know to be untrue in the book justifies doubts about the rest; and what I know to be true of Toscanini on the one hand, and of Chotzinoff on the other hand, makes the book not charming, for me, but abominable. Actually some readers, even without knowledge, were able to perceive, when the book appeared in 1956, that it was damaging not only to Toscanini but to Chotzinoff: that it was hardly admirable of Chotzinoff, when he had found it advantageous to do so, to have accepted mistreatment he could have chosen not to accept, and now, with Toscanini still alive, to reveal his bad behavior to the public, destroying the privacy of his personal life that he had trusted a friend to preserve.

I didn't ever know Chotzinoff—by choice: I declined Virgil Thomson's invitation to join the New York Music Critics' Circle when he organized it, because I didn't want anything to do with Chotzinoff and some of the others; and when I began to attend Toscanini's rehearsals at NBC in 1942 I told Walter Toscanini: "I don't meet Mr. Chotzinoff." Clearly this couldn't have been because of anything he had done to me; and actually it was because of what he had done to others. Not what he had done in his early years with his lifeless piano accompaniments to the performances of Alma Gluck and Efrem Zimbalist, or Jascha Heifetz; but what he had done to musicians with his writing when he had become music critic of the New York *World* in the mid-twenties. Not only did he begin without any standing as a critic, but he quickly revealed his lack of any capacities for the job; and his way of achieving standing with his readers and impressing them with his capacities was to act "this hard-boiled scribe" (as he referred to himself) whom nothing could fool and very little could impress—the marvelous *Lieder*-singer Elena Gerhardt being the one I recall now of the numerous musicians Chotzinoff stepped on to make himself look big. After the death of *The World* he went to *The Post*, which published a page of congratulatory statements on the appointment by musical celebrities; and though I wasn't asked, I wrote in *Hound & Horn* that it was a calamity, "for in place of the judgment, intelligence and courage that are so urgently needed, he contributes a sneer." In 1936 Sarnoff brought him into NBC; and his friendship with Toscanini enabled him to secure Toscanini for NBC and to handle him for the company, in which he was given the position of musical counsel.

Chotzinoff and his falsehoods would be something to forget, if it were not for their connection with, and impact on, one of the great geniuses of the century—the fact that they were themselves some of the realities, and enable us to see other realities, hidden behind the public operation of this genius that was visible. The rehearsals at which his explosion of rage occurred can be considered part of that public operation; and here one finds that the NBC Symphony musicians forgave him because they understood that the outbursts had behind them no personal motivation or animus, but only an obsessed musician's unbearable frustration over the orchestra's momentary failure to produce what he wanted. Moreover, "after the rehearsal—or when you'd go out to his home," said one of these musicians, "he was sweet, like a child. I loved the Old Man; and I think everybody did." This is not the image most people have of Toscanini; but they *will* recognize the man described by that NBC musician's further statement: "You knew that as a man he had principle and character: what he felt was right was right; and you could kill him but it would still be right. It was like a cat: you can't make a cat do anything: he's got courage and guts ... You knew Toscanini couldn't be pulled or swayed by management—that if NBC didn't do what he liked he'd stay home: for $6,000 a concert he'd tell them to go to hell." There was this appearance of power and independence, and not just the appearance but the reality. But on occasion, what Toscanini couldn't be made to do, he could be got to do by other methods.

What the NBC Symphony musician referred to in his statement that "for $6,000 a concert he'd tell them to go to hell" was Toscanini's absenting himself from NBC the season of 1941-42, when he conducted the Philadelphia Orchestra a few times and made some recordings of the performances. None of these was issued until 1963, when at long last the recording of Schubert's

C-major was released by RCA Victor. Several months before its release it was broadcast by WFMT in Chicago and WRVR in New York, with an introduction by the critic of the Chicago *Sun-Times*, who, speaking with his usual pretensions to intimate knowledge he didn't have, gave this explanation of how Toscanini happened to be conducting the Philadelphia Orchestra in 1941-42: "When you hired Arturo Toscanini to be musical director of an orchestra, you got a real musical director—one who felt that among other responsibilities his was the job of hiring and firing guest conductors;" so that when NBC in 1941 "engaged for the summer concerts one conductor whom Toscanini felt was not suitable . . . he refused to return for the winter season of 1941-42 . . ." It was the story he had been told by those who didn't want to tell him the true reason for Toscanini's absenting himself: the situation which reached an explosive climax on the last Friday in December 1940. Several NBC musicians told me what happened that day; here is one such account:

> It took him some time to discover that the orchestra NBC said it created for him played in other programs under other conductors; and it made him angry because it affected our work with him. On a Friday in December 1940 we were scheduled to rehearse from 5 to 7:30 in Carnegie Hall for a performance of the *Missa Solemnis* the next night. There was a concert of the Chicago Symphony in Carnegie Hall that afternoon, after which the platform had to be set up on the stage for the chorus in the *Missa*; so the rehearsal didn't start until 5:30, which meant it would go on to 8. But thirty-five men of the orchestra had to play with Frank Black in the Cities Service program in Studio 8H at 8; and they had to leave at 7:30 if they were to pack their instruments, get to 8H, change their clothes, and be ready for the broadcast at 8. And since this was the first time we were doing the *Missa* with Maestro he was really out to work. So 7:30 came, and he kept right on working; then it was 7:32, and 7:33, and at that point the personnel manager stood behind Maestro and signalled to the men one by one to sneak out. I saw Carlton Cooley, right under Maestro's nose, get down on his hands and knees and crawl out; and it was only after a number of men had done this that the Old Man's eye caught the movement of the bassoon that one of the men was holding as he

crawled out, and he discovered what had been going on. He was so infuriated that he threw down his stand and walked out. He conducted the performance the next night and finished his series that season; but a couple of months later when the conductors for 1941-42 were announced, he was not among them.

It is interesting after this to read Chotzinoff's version of the incident in his book. Toscanini's demands, he writes on p. 108, sometimes interfered with the operations of the commercial programs that earned the cost of the NBC Symphony broadcasts; and to illustrate he writes that when it was not working with Toscanini the orchestra was assigned to those commercial programs, adding that it could however play only a few, since seventy-five or eighty percent of its working time each week was required by Toscanini's rehearsals and broadcast. And on one occasion Chotzinoff scheduled the usual two-and-a-half-hour rehearsal for a performance of Verdi's *Requiem* in Carnegie Hall at 4, to make sure that if Toscanini ran over the two and a half hours there would be ample time for thirty of the men to get to NBC at 8 for the commercial program they had to play. But after three and a half hours, Toscanini—who "knew nothing about the '*commerziale*' and would have cared less ... had he known"—gave no sign of ending the rehearsal; so Chotzinoff had to instruct the personnel manager to signal to the men to sneak out. And though Toscanini made a scene when he discovered what was happening, the next day he recognized the men's need of the extra income from the commercial program, and all was well again.

Every detail in Chotzinoff's account is untrue—including the one that Toscanini knew nothing about the commercial program. It wasn't in his mind while he was rehearsing; but he did know about it and did care about it. As the NBC musician said, it had taken him some time to discover that the men of his orchestra had to play in other programs, and the discovery had angered him. Chotzinoff not only had foreseen that anger but had feared he might even refuse to come if he knew the truth, and had been careful to conceal it from him, as he is careful to conceal it from the readers of his book until his mention of it in connection with the rehearsal incident on p. 108. On p. 79 he writes that he told Toscanini in Milan NBC "would built him a great orchestra"—which conveyed to Toscanini what it conveyed twenty-five years later to Eugene Lyons, who in his biography of Sarnoff writes that Chotzinoff told Toscanini NBC "would create a great orchestra especially for him." And Chotzinoff's further statements on pp. 84-86—that on his return to New York he "started to put together an orchestra;" that a symphony orchestra is not built in a day, and "we had only ten months in which to assemble one;" that by November 1937 "we had assembled a superb body of men"—these statements imply that, starting from zero, he engaged for NBC all the members of an additional new orchestra for Toscanini. Moreover, he makes the implied claim explicit on p. 86: when Toscanini cabled his withdrawal from the project because he had heard it was costing some NBC men their jobs, Chotzinoff cabled in reply that far from costing even one man his job, Toscanini's engagement had caused NBC "to take on . . . a full symphony orchestra . . ."

In all this there isn't the slightest hint of the true facts that were given in the *Fortune* article: that NBC's contract with the musicians' union for 1938 had required it to increase its staff orchestra from seventy-four to 115 men; that the ninety-two men constituting the NBC Symphony were part of that staff orchestra of 115; that those ninety-two comprised thirty-one men retained from the 1937 staff orchestra, and sixty-one men whom Chotzinoff had engaged as higher-caliber replacements of members of the 1937 staff orchestra (who *had*, then, lost their jobs) and as additions for the 1938 staff orchestra; and that of the thirty hours which the ninety-two were obligated to work during the week, only fifteen were allotted to Toscanini's rehearsals and broadcast, and the remaining fifteen went to other NBC programs, sustaining and commercial.

This fact—that the orchestra built "for him" was actually playing half its working time with other conductors—Chotzinoff, as I said earlier, had concealed from Toscanini because he had known Toscanini would object to it, and why he would object: the other conductors were unable to hold the players to his technical and musical standards of performance, so that his work in disciplining and teaching the orchestra was constantly being undone; and many of the men came to his rehearsal on Friday after several hours' work with Walter Damrosch for that morning's music appreciation program and with Frank Black for that evening's Cities Service program. The result of Chotzinoff's concealment was that week after week Toscanini was baffled and frustrated and exasperated by the strange fact that the orchestra which delighted him with its youthful energy on other days played like "tired old men" on Friday. Only after some time did he discover why; and it was his growing anger about it that boiled over in response to the crowning outrage at the *Requiem* rehearsal. And far from all being well again the next day, it impelled him to absent himself from NBC the next year.

He did so because this time he discovered what had been concealed; but he didn't every time. In July 1947 the NBC Symphony broadcasts were moved, for the season of 1947-48, from Sunday at 5 to Saturday at 6:30. (NBC had been unable to get a commercial sponsor for the NBC Symphony, and Ford wanted to buy Sunday at 5 for another program.) I pointed out in my *Music on the Radio* column in the Sunday *Herald Tribune*— which Toscanini read—that the new time was one when people were busy with their children and their dinners and unable to listen; and a few weeks later I published objections to the new time from readers. The change was made in October for the last few broadcasts of the NBC Summer Symphony; and a couple of weeks before the start of Toscanini's winter series in November I visited him.

After we had been talking for some time he said suddenly: "Is very interesting: they say only seven million listen to NBC Symphony on Sunday, but eleven million listen on Saturday."

Since nobody could be listening to his broadcasts that hadn't even begun, I asked: "How do they know that?"

"NBC make investigation," he said.

Again, NBC couldn't have "investigated" how many people were listening to the broadcasts that hadn't begun; so I asked "Who told you that?"

"Chotzinoff."

In its July announcement NBC had said a greater number of stations would carry the program on Saturday at 6:30 (I pointed out that this was because the time was not commercially valuable, since many people couldn't listen); and it probably had estimated from the number of stations a potential eleven million as the number of people who would be listening. If one had pressed Chotzinoff he undoubtedly would have said he was referring to this advance estimate; but he apparently had given Toscanini the impression that NBC had conducted a survey of a kind which had enabled it to establish eleven million as the number of actual listeners; and this caused Toscanini to accept a change of time which cost him part of his audience, and which he would have objected to, and might even have refused to accept, if he had understood the real nature of the "investigation". The incident was in effect a betrayal of his interest by someone he had trusted not to betray him.

And the final betrayal was the malicious and largely false book that Chotzinoff published after the end of the NBC Symphony had brought a termination of his relation with Toscanini, who considered him one of those responsible for the destruction of his beloved orchestra, and when there was nothing more to gain from Toscanini. The book was only one of the penalties Toscanini paid for having people like Chotzinoff around him.

ACKNOWLEDGEMENTS

In the production of the first edition of this book I was indebted to

Walter Toscanini, for verification of a number of dates and programs and information about his father's early repertory; and for his permission to publish the texts of two of his father's letters, which, however, were not published in the first edition (1959) of this book because the necessary permissions of others were not received.

Several members of the NBC Symphony, and other persons who also had to remain nameless, for information about some matters I discussed.

Robert Hupka, for making available to me a few of his photographs of Toscanini in action.

Robert E. Garis, Roger Dakin, Margaret Nicholson and Charles B. Farrell, for editorial assistance.

In the production of this second edition I am indebted to

Ben Raeburn of Horizon Press, for his wish to bring out the new edition, and for yet another collaboration of a kind that is unique in my experience.

Robert Hupka, for again making his photographs available to me.

Mary Ann Youngren, for her comments and suggestions on the new material.

Wally Toscanini (Countess Castelbarco) and Walfredo Toscanini, for their permission to publish the two letters of Arturo Toscanini; and Emanuela di Castelbarco, for her assistance in this matter.

Thomas Hathaway and Michael Gray, for information about records in German RCA's *Toscanini Edition*.